HAUNTED ALABAMA BLACK BELT

DAVID HIGDON & BRETT TALLEY

Haunted America

Published by Haunted America
A Division of The History Press
Charleston, SC 29403
www.historypress.net

Cover image: Front view of Brownstone Manor. *Courtesy Faith Serafin.*

First published 2013

Manufactured in the United States

ISBN 978.1.60949.944.0

Library of Congress CIP data applied for.

Notice: The information in this book is true and complete to the best of our knowledge. It is offered without guarantee on the part of the authors or The History Press. The authors and The History Press disclaim all liability in connection with the use of this book.

Kathryn Tucker Windham,
the *American storyteller*

June 2, 1918–June 12, 2011

CONTENTS

Acknowledgements

The authors would like to thank the innumerable people who helped to make this book possible, from the people who agreed to share their stories to the friends and family members who supported us throughout the process of writing the book. We couldn't have done it without you, and this book is truly as much a testament to you as it is to us.

Still, some people deserve special recognition. David would like to thank his wife, Debbie, who has stood beside him through good times and bad, and his four children, who have inspired him to pursue this project.

As for Brett, he would like his parents, Mike and Sue Talley, to know that this book is for them. They inspired his love of history and his desire to always seek the truth. He would be nothing without them, and this book is but one part of his life that he was only able to accomplish because of their love. Brett would also like to dedicate this book to his nephew, Cristian. Read, learn and remember.

Both authors would like to give a special thanks to Faith Serafin, the author of the wonderful *Haunted Auburn and Opelika*, *Haunted Columbus, Georgia: Phantoms of the Fountain City* and *Haunted Montgomery: Ghost Stories from the Heart of Dixie*. Faith's knowledge of the haunted history of Alabama is matched only by her kindness and willingness to help us in our efforts. We could not have done this without her.

Traditional Counties of the Alabama Black Belt

A view of the Alabama Black Belt.

INTRODUCTION

There is a place in Alabama, a region that stretches across its lower-middle, from Georgia to Mississippi. It is a place steeped in history—a place where a people were enslaved, a nation broken and a new dream of freedom born. It is a place where the past is always near at hand. Sometimes, that past takes a moment to whisper in your ear. They call this place the "Black Belt."

In 1814, forces under the command of Andrew Jackson defeated an alliance of Creek Indians, opening much of the territory of Alabama to settlement. And come the settlers did. When they poured across the Appalachian Mountains and made their way down to the plains of the South, to the flat fields that stretch all the way to the sea, the new inhabitants of the state discovered something unusual. The soil was different here. Instead of the red clay that characterizes the northern part of Alabama, the farmers found a thin layer of dark, rich earth. From that soil would grow massive fortunes, a war that would cost hundreds of thousands of lives and a movement that would set a people free.

Everyone knows that cotton was king in the antebellum South, and nowhere was that more true than the Black Belt of Alabama. With deep wells to provide needed water, mighty mansions rose throughout the region, engaging thousands of African slaves to grow the crop that made the owners of those plantations wealthy and powerful. They used that wealth and power to ensure that on January 11, 1861, Alabama followed South Carolina, Mississippi and Florida in seceding from the Union. So iconic was the Black

Belt in the antebellum South that Montgomery, the city at the heart of the region, was declared the capital of the new nation. The "Buckle of the Black Belt" had become the "Cradle of the Confederacy."

The war that followed didn't quite go the way the men and women of lower Alabama might have expected. The Black Belt was spared much of the suffering of the rest of the South, though, and by the time Farragut's fleet entered Mobile and Union soldiers started making their way north, the war was all but over. With the conflict's end, a group of people was free and a way of life shattered. But while slavery passed away, the world's thirst for cotton did not ebb, and the millions of newly freed slaves needed employment. Sharecropping was born, a system that bound the poor—both black and white—to the land almost as tightly as the chains of slavery had previously. A place named for its soil would keep its moniker because of the people who worked it. And the system of racial discrimination that grew up around the region set up the next great battle for freedom and equality.

For nearly one hundred years, that system—known as Jim Crow—held sway. Then, on December 1, 1955, four African Americans were sitting on a crowded afternoon bus in downtown Montgomery. The driver asked them to get up so that white riders could have their seats. Three of them complied. One of them did not. When the police arrested Rosa Parks, they could not have known that it was the beginning of the end of segregation.

The fight for racial equality was waged as much in the Black Belt as anywhere else in America. It was here where the Montgomery Bus Boycott—spurred by Rosa Parks's act of courage—ended discrimination against blacks in public transit. It was here where Freedom Riders, including members of President John F. Kennedy's Department of Justice, were beaten by angry mobs opposed to integration. It was here where protestors, led by Martin Luther King Jr., marched from Montgomery to Selma seeking the right to vote. And it was here where brave men and women—black and white, northern and southern—joined forces to ensure that institutionalized racism and discrimination would forever be consigned to the dustbin of history.

In a place like that, a place that has seen so much history, struggle and suffering, as well as so many tears and triumphs, is it any surprise that there are those who believe that some events are burned forever into the very fabric of the Black Belt? Stories abound of cemeteries where the dead do not sleep, of courthouses haunted by the unjustly accused, of plantations with ghosts as thick as cotton, of libraries that retain more than old books and of hotels where the guests never check out. In Alabama's Black Belt, the nights are heavy with the past, and history sometimes finds its way into the present.

PROLOGUE
KATHRYN TUCKER WINDHAM HOUSE

It would not do to talk of ghosts and ghouls and things that go bump in the night in the Black Belt of Alabama without paying special tribute to the house of Kathryn Tucker Windham and the woman who lived within it. Kathryn Tucker was born in the summer of 1918 to James and Helen in the town of Selma. Her father was a man who could spin a yarn, and whether by biology or bequeathing, Kathryn was an apple that did not fall far from the tree. When the Second World War came, Kathryn took her Huntingdon education and put it to good use, replacing a male reporter at the *Birmingham News* who had gone off to fight. It was the last time she would need such luck; talent, as they say, will win out.

She married Amasa Windham soon after the war, raising their three children in Selma while she worked for seemingly more newspapers and various publications than could be contained in this meager volume. Years passed, and Kathryn continued to build a reputation as a writer of great repute. And then came October 1966 and the haunting that would make her famous around the world.

Kathryn told it that she was sitting in her living room reading a book on a bright, sunny day. The door opened, and she heard heavy footsteps tromping through the house. She assumed it was her son, come home from Birmingham Southern. She called out to him, but got no response. She called a little bit louder. Still nothing. When she got up to see, there was no one in the house. It was only the first time of many that she'd hear those footsteps walking down the hall, but the only household member the spirit ever frightened was the old family cat. The family decided to call their new friend Jeffrey.

They heard him often, and sometimes they'd find things out of place, but they never saw him until some friends of the family decided to pull out the old Ouija board and see if they could make a special connection to the spirit. Alas, they failed to make contact—or so they thought. When the photos from that night were developed, a dark, shadowy figure appeared in the background, one that had the distinctive outline of a human being. When Windham saw the photos, she immediately became obsessed. She called a friend of a friend, Margaret Gillis Figh, a local expert on ghost stories and folklore. When the two connected, a perfect partnership was formed, and the idea for *13 Alabama Ghosts and Jeffrey* was born.

Windham went on to write seven books of true ghost stories before she passed away in 2011. And in the process, she would become a legend, a storyteller of the finest degree, a master of the old ways of spinning a yarn. Jeffrey was always with her, although he never appeared in "the flesh" again. The service she did to the people of Alabama and other areas of the South cannot be overstated. Who can say if some of the ghost stories she preserved would have been forgotten if she had never put them down on paper? And what a tragedy it would have been to lose that history.

If the reader would indulge us, Brett would like to tell his own story about Kathryn Tucker Windham and how this wonderful woman affected his life, just as she did so many others throughout the state of Alabama and our nation.

It was late in the last decade of the last century, 1999 or perhaps even 2000, when Mrs. Windham came to Bevill State Community College, a place of learning located across the street from my high school. Having spent my childhood sitting at the figurative knee of Windham as she spun her tales of ghosts that haunt tucked-away places all over the Southeast, I was very enthusiastic about hearing her speak and having the opportunity to listen to her weave a story firsthand. I went with a friend, and eager children that we were, we sat in the front row next to a kindly old lady. We struck up a conversation with the lady, and at some point, my friend asked if she had heard of Kathryn Tucker Windham. "Why yes," she answered politely. "Yeah," my friend said, "I just hope she's not boring." The old woman laughed. "Son," she said, "I certainly hope you're right. She's me!"

My friend, of course, was mortified. But Mrs. Windham seemed more concerned about him than any hurt feelings she might have had about not being recognized. But by all indications and evidence, that was the kind of person Kathryn Tucker Windham was.

Windham once said that she figured people were so interested in what happened in the world beyond our own because you could never really know what happens after death. We may have faith, yes, but faith of things unseen. It's the final mystery, one that Mrs. Windham has now gone on to unveil. And I'd like to think that she finally met Jeffrey face to face.

Part I
Eastern Black Belt

Barbour County

With a population of just over twenty-seven thousand, one might not expect much from tiny Barbour County, nestled in the southeast corner of Alabama. And yet no fewer than eight of Alabama's governors—including the infamous George Wallace—called the county home. If one drives through Barbour County and looks at the great homes of towns like Eufaula, such a fact is probably less surprising. The migrants who came to settle the former Creek Indian territories found rich soil, ripe for the planting of cotton. The county soon became home to the state's elite. Great mansions were built, the pride of the men and women who lived there. If some stories are to be believed, the owners of those homes never left them, even in death.

The Cato-Thorn House

In Barbour County, the cream of southern aristocracy is on display, and one will find the kind of Greek Revival antebellum mansions that some might expect to exist only within the confines of a Hollywood film. Built just before the start of the Civil War, the Cato-Thorn House was the brainchild of Lewis Llewellyn Cato. Its most striking feature is the cupola rising from the

Front view of the Cato-Thorne House. *Courtesy Amanda Baird/BlackDoll Photography.*

center of the roof. Look closely, and it becomes apparent that the cupola is an almost exact replica, in miniature, of the house itself.

When Alabama voted to secede, a huge party was held at the home. William Lowndes Yancey, one of the leading secessionists in the state, is said to have given a rousing speech in support of independence. When the house was renovated in the 1970s, a trunk containing letters from Confederate president Jefferson Davis and other significant figures of the Civil War was found in the attic.

The Confederacy is strong in the Cato-Thorn House, and perhaps it's no surprise that its spirits come from that era as well. Some speculate that it was the restoration that stirred them up. Several of the painters who worked on the house reported the uneasy feeling that they were being watched. It was only when one of them looked up to the landing above and saw a man standing there, clothed in the full dress uniform of a Confederate officer, that these suspicions were confirmed. The painter left that day and never returned.

And it's not just the men of the era who have come back to visit the house. A previous owner named Victoria is said to also remain on the premises. She has been seen dressed in the full regalia of a woman of the antebellum age.

Victoria herself had a ghost story she liked to tell visitors. She had a dog that lived with her in the house. It seemed that something she could not see was scaring the dog, and it would often run through the house until it was exhausted. Finally, Victoria went to the second floor of the house, where the activity seemed to be centered, and told the ghost that it was welcome to stay but that it had to quit chasing the dog. The chasing stopped, the dog quit running and all of them lived together without incident. To this day, the people who own the Cato-Thorn House have been known to say that the first floor belongs to them, while the second floor belongs to the ghost. An equitable arrangement, indeed.

Kendall Manor

Another of Eufaula's odes to days long gone by—to days of king cotton and steamships and of an age when southern Alabama was the wealthiest region in the nation—is the Kendall Manor. This is a gorgeous two-story mansion in the Italianate style. Sitting on a hill and crowned by a cupola that overseers could use to monitor both slaves working in the cotton fields and steamboat traffic coming up and down the Chattahoochee River, the owners of Kendall Manor must have felt like the entire town of Eufaula was their own kingdom to survey.

The town of Eufaula gets its name from one of the Indian tribes that used to call the area home. Meaning "high bluff" in the Muscogee language, the embankments overlooking the river and the fertile cropland fed by regular floods quickly drew white settlers to the area. Houses like Kendall Manor were built as monuments to the wealth and prosperity that followed. Soon the town had become a major shipping and trading mecca, with traders and merchants from all over Georgia and Alabama drawn to the bustling city.

But it wasn't just the fertile land that made Eufaula wealthy. Someone had to work that land, and it was that need for labor that brought thousands of African slaves to the area. When the question of secession to protect that way of life became a pressing one after the election of Abraham Lincoln, the wealthy and powerful of the area, called the Eufaula Regency, were adamant supporters of separation. When the Civil War began, the people of Eufaula answered the call for soldiers, and many from the area would fight in some of the biggest battles of the war.

What the people of the town could not know is that they had signed the death warrant for the glory days of the Black Belt. The war, which started with many promising victories for Confederate forces, soon turned against the South. When Montgomery fell in early 1865, there was nothing to stand between federal troops and the town of Eufaula. Given that many of the towns that fell to the Union were burned to the ground, the people of Eufaula prepared for the worst. When a messenger arrived with word that four thousand Union cavalrymen were moving in their direction, it seemed that all hope was lost.

But luck was on their side. With Union troops across the river and in sight of the city, news came of the surrender of Robert E. Lee at Appomattox Court House, as well as Joe Johnston's capitulation to William Tecumseh Sherman in Raleigh, North Carolina. Under a flag of truce, Union troops crossed the river and marched into the city, peacefully and without incident. Unlike so many of the great cities of the South, Eufaula survived the war without death and destruction.

But things would never be like they were before the war. Even as new rail lines and cotton mills brought a measure of prosperity back to the town, places like Kendall Manor watched as the world passed them by. But while Eufaula isn't as wealthy as it once was, it is one of the most historic cities in the country. And Kendall Manor is one of more than seven hundred buildings in Eufaula listed on the National Register of Historic Places.

Front view of the Kendall Manor. *Courtesy Amanda Baird/BlackDoll Photography.*

A little bit of that history remains at Kendall Manor. It often seems like every house in Eufaula is haunted, and Kendall is no different. The manor's particular ghost is called Annie. She was, a very long time ago, a nursemaid who cared for generations of children who passed through the halls of Kendall. It is said that she was very protective of the children and rather strict in their upbringing. Annie has long since passed from the scene, but her spirit remains, and it is said to appear whenever there are children in her area who are acting up and need discipline. And if anything would keep kids in line, seeing a ghost is probably it.

We know less about the other story attached to Kendall Manor. It involves a spirit that is said to ride a white horse. When danger is about, or when something tragic and horrible is about to happen, the man on the white horse appears at Kendall Manor, a harbinger of doom. Let's hope that's a spirit you never encounter.

The Shorter Mansion

The Shorter Mansion is a testament to the nostalgia for days gone by, but perhaps not the one you expect. While Shorter appears to the world to be a classic antebellum home, it was actually built after the war, in 1884 to be exact. Eli Sims Shorter II and his wife, Wileyna Lamar Shorter, constructed the house to be a modest townhome for their family. But renovations commenced in 1901—forty years after the Civil War began—to transform it into a magnificent Greek Revival mansion. So convincing was the effort that the mansion was even included in the film *Sweet Home Alabama*.

The family lived in the house until 1965, when the great-granddaughter decided to move to Atlanta. The people of Eufaula loved the house so much that they pooled their money and bought the house for the city heritage association. With it, they may have also purchased a ghost.

Those who claim to know say that the Shorter Mansion is haunted by the ghost of a man, although who he is no one knows. They call him the "man in the top hat," and apparently he has a habit of appearing in wedding photos. A top hat is on display in the mansion, one that belonged to Governor Sparks of Alabama. Is he the spirit that haunts the home? It's hard to say. In any event, the crew members at the Shorter Mansion make sure that they always show examples of these photos to anyone who decides to book the mansion for a wedding, just so they know they can expect an extra guest.

Front view of the Shorter Mansion. *Courtesy Amanda Baird/BlackDoll Photography.*

Then there is the lady in pink. While she is also in the habit of appearing in wedding pictures, she has surfaced in real life as well. While a tour was going on in the Shorter Mansion, one of the staff was talking with a woman in the parlor. At least, *she* was talking. The other woman never said a word, merely nodding her head at appropriate times. The staff member turned away for but a moment, and when she looked back, the woman had simply vanished.

Shorter Mansion is definitely an ode to the past, both living and dead.

Fendall Hall

When Edward and Anna Young arrived in Eufaula in 1837, they came to a town that was in the midst of the cotton boom that swept through the South in the prewar era. They were the owners of slaves, and they drew their wealth from the efforts of those in chains. In fact, Fendall Hall was not named such until the middle of the twentieth century. Until that time, it was known simply as the "house on the hill." Perhaps, then, it is appropriate that the family completed the gorgeous Italianate mansion in 1860, on the eve of the Civil War. It would play its part in that war, used as a temporary hospital for men wounded in the fighting that led to the burning of Atlanta.

But despite the losses and depravations caused by the war, the Young family managed to hang on to the home all the way until the 1970s, when it was finally purchased by the Alabama Historical Commission. Today, the house serves the people of Eufaula, giving back to the descendants of many of the people who built it. And depending on whom you believe, it also serves as a home for the deceased.

It is said by some that Fendall Hall never feels empty. Doors open and close, cold spots are frequently felt and apparitions appear and disappear at random. Some have seen a young woman running toward the house, only to vanish when she reaches the door. Others report a young boy who watches guests in the foyer from the upstairs banister. And while most of the visitors to Fendall are not bothered by the presence at the house, others feel quite differently about it. There are some who report a sense of being unwanted, as if whoever remains behind is displeased with the disturbance.

The caretakers of Fendall Hall have attempted to research the history of the home in the hopes of better understanding the source of these spirits. So far, their efforts have failed. Whatever goes on at Fendall Hall truly is a mystery.

Front view of Fendall Hall. *Courtesy Amanda Baird/BlackDoll Photography.*

Bullock County

Bullock County is named for Colonel Edward C. Bullock—the primogenitor of actress Sandra Bullock—who left Barbour County to settle the land to its northwest. Union Springs, the sort of idyllic place one expects to find in the small-town South, serves as its county seat. It boasts one of the oldest jails in the state and a 150-year old hotel, the Josephine. A passer-through no doubt leaves Union Springs enchanted, with no notion of the dark mysteries bubbling just below the surface.

Bullock County Courthouse

The Bullock County Courthouse simply looks like it should be haunted. Its two towers of red brick loom over a colonnaded central structure that seems to brood over visitors, daring them to stay awhile. Within hangs the faded photo of a Civil War soldier, his eyes watching you every step you take. That photo alone has unnerved generations of those who work within the courthouse doors, to the point that one former sheriff had the old portrait covered up. The elevators go up and down with no cause

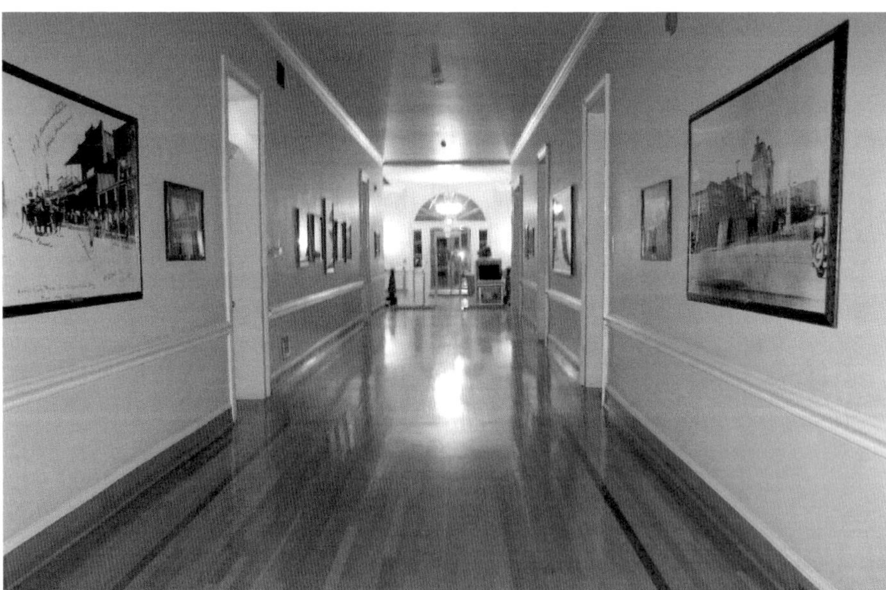

Hallway of Bullock County Courthouse. *Courtesy Faith Serafin.*

Front view of Bullock County Courthouse. *Courtesy Faith Serafin.*

or explanation, and more than once, the footsteps or whispered words of disembodied voices have floated down the halls to greet the ears of someone supposedly alone.

The courthouse was built in 1871, its designers placing it in an idyllic setting, surrounded by a park and gazebo. It is patterned after an executive office in Washington, D.C., although no one can ever agree on which one. But whatever the case, cameras rarely work in the Bullock County Courthouse, and when they do, the pictures are often oddly blurred and indistinct. Batteries drain within the confines of the building, and an uneasy feeling seems to hang over the courtroom itself.

What happened here to cause these bizarre occurrences? Did someone die here? Did a trial end in an unjust conviction? Like so many questions that remain about the haunted places of the earth, we simply do not know.

Pauly Jail

While the Bullock County Courthouse was designed to be a beautiful and imposing building, the Pauly Jail was constructed with more practical considerations in mind. Finished in 1897, the jail is one of the oldest in the

Left: Pauly Jail ground floor.
Courtesy Faith Serafin.

Below: Front view of Pauly Jail.
Courtesy Faith Serafin.

state, if not the oldest. The jail is of an interesting design. It is a three-story, red brick structure that—with its spikes and turrets—reminds one more of a castle than a place of incarceration. Today, the jail serves as a museum of sorts to the facility's primary goal in the days of its operation: combating the persistent and pervasive moonshine industry in the forests around the city.

The second floor of the jail features a trapdoor. One might wonder why, until you realize that it was in this place where the men condemned to die within Pauly's walls would meet the hangman. Down went the trapdoor, and down the men followed. Death came quickly. But that doesn't mean that everyone who died within Pauly went quietly, and some of their voices can still be heard.

There aren't that many aspects of a paranormal haunting that aren't present at the Pauly Jail. Cold spots in the middle of summer. The sound of footsteps down empty hallways. Thumps and bangs and things that go bump in the night, followed by shadowy figures that can't be explained. Is Pauly Jail haunted? The moans of the dead executed within its walls certainly seem to say yes.

The Josephine Hotel

For more than 130 years, the Josephine Hotel has stood watch over the town of Union Springs. Oh, what mysteries it has seen: the grand masquerade balls that were held there, the exquisite dinners hosting the wealthy and well-to-do from all over the region…and the spirits that still haunt its halls.

Josephine Hotel staircase. *Courtesy Faith Serafin.*

Built in 1880, the hotel was constructed by Dr. Joseph Fleming. He named the hotel after his beloved wife, Josephine. Its thirty-two rooms were considered some of the finest in Alabama. The hotel was a center of commerce in Union Springs, with merchants often coming within its doors to sell their wares. The saloon on the bottom floor was always lively, and

Front view of the Josephine Hotel. *Courtesy Faith Serafin.*

if you wanted to see the most important people in Alabama, the Josephine was a fine place to do it.

But like all things, the heyday of the Josephine came and went. The grand hotel passed from one owner to another, and soon it fell into disrepair. Only now is it in the process of being restored to its former glory. And yet, it seems for some that the party still goes on.

Walk through the Josephine, and you will never walk alone. The smells of pipes and cigars seem to float up from the saloon below. The fine old piano on the first floor occasionally plays on its own, and whispers float down the hallways. Noises echo through the upper floors. It is said by many that the third-floor rooms hold special significance—that spirits watch from darkened corners. Few nights go by without otherworldly interruption.

For now, we can only speculate. The work of bringing the Josephine to a state where it can host the living—as well as the dead—goes on. But when opening day comes, oh what a party it will be.

DALE COUNTY

The sleepy county of Dale is likely most famous for something that happened one thousand miles away from the county line. Dale County produced the Fifteenth Alabama, perhaps the most decorated regiment from the state to fight in the Civil War. The Fifteenth would see its high-water mark in the same place as the Confederacy, in a little railroad stop in rural Pennsylvania called Gettysburg.

It was July 2, the second day of that monumental battle. The Confederate forces had fared well on the first day of the conflict, and men in gray were confident that they could gain a great victory over their Northern brethren. And what a victory it might be. Smash the Army of the Potomac here, and the path to Washington was open. The war might be over in a matter of weeks. But first they needed the high ground, and that meant taking Little Round Top.

On the summit of that prominence that overlooked the rest of the battlefield was the Twentieth Maine. These men understood well that their position was the linchpin of the entire Union line. If they broke, the line broke, the army was flanked and the battle would likely end in a rout. Reinforcements were coming to help them, but they weren't there yet. The men of the Alabama Regiment knew that, too.

The attack started early. The Alabamans charged up the hill, while the men of Maine tried desperately to hold their position. After nearly two hours of fighting without end, Colonel Joshua Chamberlain, the commander of the Twentieth Maine, realized that he was almost out of ammunition.

The Southern attack continued. The moment of truth was at hand. And then Chamberlain did the unthinkable: he ordered his men to fix bayonets. It's hard to imagine what the Alabamans thought when they saw it. They were so close to victory. So close to glory. And then, like madmen from some hellish dream, down the hill came the Twentieth Maine, bayonets gleaming in the afternoon sun, shrieking each and every one like banshees from across the sea.

So shocked were the Confederates by this action that their lines were broken, and many of the men were taken captive. By the time the Southern forces regrouped, reinforcements had arrived to secure Little Round Top. The Confederates were never able to take the high ground. Thus, they were never able to break the Union lines. The Battle of Gettysburg was lost for the Confederacy, and with it the war. There can be little doubt that the first stroke of the Southern surrender at Appomattox began on that hilltop with a singular act of bravery.

Sketoe's Hole

While the men of the Fifteenth Alabama served their state and their country honorably during the many battles of the Civil War, their brethren who stayed behind in Dale County did not do it such justice. In fact, it was their cruelty that led to one of the most infamous events in Alabama's history, one that gave us the story known simply as "Sketoe's Hole."

The story drifts down to us through the ages, featuring prominently in the tales of that grande dame of southern storytelling, Kathryn Tucker Windham. It begins with a man from Madrid, Spain—William Sketoe.

Bill had lived most of his life in Alabama, having moved to Dale County with his father as a boy. But that fact did not prevent the locals from viewing him with suspicious eyes. He was, after all, a Spaniard, and relations with that nation had been tenuous at best in the years following the formation of the Union. But as the boy grew, his kind manner and deep religious faith eventually earned him friends in the area, and it wasn't long before he was preaching sermons at churches around the county. He soon ended up with a congregation of his own in a little log cabin Methodist church in Newton, where he met and fell in love with his future wife.

For several years, they lived happily together. Sketoe tended to his growing flock, and it seemed as though the young couple would grow old together. But then came the War Between the States. When secession was announced, Sketoe prayed that it would not come to war. Sadly, it was not to be. The South would not compromise its position, and the North would not sacrifice the Union. War was inevitable. When it began, Sketoe was one of the first men from Dale County to join the local regiment. As much as he didn't want to leave his family, he felt a duty to this adopted home and could not turn his back. So, off to war he went.

For three years, Sketoe fought bravely in battle after battle for the Confederate army. He rose through the ranks, and more importantly, he survived without injury. He might have seen the war all the way through had it not been for a message he received on the front telling him that his beloved wife was very sick and on the verge of death.

Sketoe had few options. He could stay in the military and pray that his wife got better, but Sketoe trusted few at home in Newton to nurse her back to health. Or he could hire a substitute to fight in his place, not an uncommon choice in those days. It was not cheap—$1,000 was the going rate—but Sketoe did what he had to do. He raised the funds from his pay and savings and hired a replacement to take his place on the line. Then he hurried back to Dale County to take care of his wife.

Things went well at first. His wife was overjoyed to see her husband, and she immediately began to recover. Sketoe promised that he would not leave her until she recovered fully. And that's where his problems began.

The writing was on the wall by the winter of 1864. Early victories had turned into a string of defeats for the South, and with Ulysses S. Grant providing the kind of leadership that earlier generals had been incapable of, the Confederacy was on the verge of collapse. Social order began to fall with it. In counties around the South, so-called Home Guards were set up. Composed of men who were either too old, too physically infirm or too cowardly to fight in the military, these lawless bands made it their business to ensure that loyalty to the Confederacy was complete and punished anything they saw as less than total devotion to the cause. And when they saw Sketoe, an able-bodied man at home with his wife while the war still raged (and a foreigner at that), they decided that he was a traitor and had to be punished.

It was a cold, early winter day when the Home Guard decided to strike. As Sketoe crossed the Choctawhatchee River north of Newton, he was ambushed by six men. They dragged him into the forest and beat him before putting him in a buggy and tying a noose around his neck. Some of Sketoe's friends happened to be crossing the bridge at that time, and once they saw what was happening, they rushed back to town to collect some weapons and men to free the preacher. Sketoe's attackers knew that they didn't have much time. They took the buggy and put it under an old post oak tree, and they asked Sketoe if he had any last words. He asked if he could pray, and the men gave him this one last courtesy—at least, until they heard what he prayed for.

"Forgive them, father," is all he said. When the men heard that he was praying for them and not himself, they were enraged. They struck the horse, and it pulled the cart from underneath Sketoe, leaving him dangling in midair. But the men had miscalculated. Sketoe was a large man, and his weight pulled the branch down to the point that his feet actually touched the ground. One of the men grabbed the crutch that he had because of an old war wound and used it to dig a hole in the ground beneath Sketoe, who strangled to death over that hole before his friends could return with help. That was the end of Sketoe, but it was not the end of the story.

A dark presence started to haunt the men responsible for Sketoe's death, and it was whispered in Newton that none of them slept another full night the rest of his life—what life he had left, that is. You see, something haunted the murderers of Bill Sketoe. Whether it was his vengeful spirit or the wrath of God himself, none can say. But what we know for sure is that none of the men involved in Sketoe's lynching died a natural death.

One was killed while riding his horse underneath a post oak tree—the same kind of tree from which Sketoe was hanged—when a limb broke away and struck the man in the head, killing him instantly. Another man was killed in a riding accident when his horse went wild on a flat, unremarkable road, throwing him to the ground and then trampling him to death. Yet another man was struck by lightning. Another was found dead in the midst of a deep swamp, with no cause of death evident and certainly no explanation for why his face was contorted into a mask of terror. The other two simply disappeared, never to be seen again.

But what has never disappeared is the hole that was dug beneath the feet of Sketoe, the hole that marked the place of his death. Fill it with dirt or cover it in sand. No matter; the hole would always reappear. Even one hundred years later, if you went down to the river and knew where to look, you'd find the hole, just as it had been on that fateful day so long ago.

They finally found a way to cover the hole, burying it under tons of rock as part of the construction of a bridge over the Choctawhatchee River. But one has to wonder if deep beneath its rocky cover, the hole remains, a silent sentinel to the man who died for the woman he loved.

MACON COUNTY

Macon County was settled, like so much of the land in the Black Belt, in order to grow the cotton that had made fortunes for planter families across the South. As such, it has to this day a high population of African Americans. And so it is probably not surprising that one of the most famous African American institutions of higher learning is located there: Tuskegee University.

Founded by the celebrated educator Booker T. Washington, Tuskegee taught generations of African American students—starting with freed slaves and sharecroppers—how to rise in a society that was often hostile to them. Tuskegee University was at the center of numerous notable events over the more than a century in which it has been in business. The famed inventor and botanist George Washington Carver called the university home. In 1941, the U.S. Army Air Corps established a training ground in Tuskegee for African American airmen. In one of the most remarkable incidents at the school, First Lady Eleanor Roosevelt flew with C. Alfred Anderson—a black instructor at the school—in a flight that helped to establish the legitimacy of the black aircrews. Squadrons of Tuskegee graduates—called Red Tails for the flamboyantly decorated tail sections of their fighters—performed with high distinction in the European Theater. Winning hundreds of medals, destroying dozens of enemy aircraft and losing a startlingly low number of bombers under their escort (in fact, some sources claim they never lost a plane), the success of the Red Tails went far in combating the segregationist theory that blacks were somehow inferior to their white brethren.

Grey Columns

When William Varner came to Macon County, Alabama, he decided to build a house that would embody the glory of southern wealth. Using his vast fortune and Harvard degree, he is said to have designed the house himself. The two-story, colonnaded structure is crowned with an octagonal cupola, and the veranda is framed by eighteen Doric columns. He named it Grey Columns.

Today, the house is the home of the Tuskegee University president, but it only remains to be enjoyed by the people of Tuskegee because of a quirk of fate. As we have seen throughout this book, the Union advance through southern Alabama played a critical role in the history of most of the buildings in the area, and Grey Columns is no exception.

When Union troops arrived in Tuskegee, they had every intention of burning Grey Columns to the ground. But when the commander of those troops entered the house, he found Ed Varner, scion of the Varner family, recuperating from wounds he had received in battle. In an unbelievable coincidence that bespeaks the brother-against-brother nature of the war, it turned out that the Union officer and Ed had been fraternity brothers while in college at Yale. The two men embraced, and the Union troops withdrew from the house, leaving it undisturbed and posting guards to ensure its protection. Because of the connection between the two men, much of Tuskegee was spared destruction as well.

While much of the South was laid to waste, Grey Columns attained a measure of fame in the years after the war. Such was the majesty of the home that the front gates were actually used in the movie *Gone with the Wind*. But that's not the only reason Grey Columns is famous. The ghost that haunts its halls plays a part, as well.

They say that in the days well before the Civil War, the master of the house had a dalliance with a young slave girl. That it wasn't uncommon at the time makes it no less abhorrent, but the story only gets worse. The girl

Front view of Grey Columns. *Courtesy Faith Serafin.*

fell pregnant. She knew the fate that awaited her child. Half-white did not mean half-free, and the baby would grow up as a slave unless something was done. She begged the master to grant freedom, if not to her then at least to the child. He refused. The poor girl felt that she had no choice. She didn't want her child to face the same fate as her, so she killed herself.

They say that her spirit still lingers at Grey Columns, that it walks the halls of the resplendent mansion and that its soft cries and woeful moans still echo across the grounds. She is a reminder that while there was much beauty in the antebellum South, it covered a darkness that must never be forgotten.

Tuskegee Army Airfield

Today, there are few who have not heard of the Tuskegee Airmen, the famed Red Tails of World War II. These African American pilots shattered the preconceived notions of a nation that was rife with discrimination. Because of their extraordinary efforts in the European Theater, the Tuskegee Airmen took one more step toward equality.

But it's not as if they were born flying. Someone had to teach them. That education was conducted at the Tuskegee Army Airfield. The field, built

Front view of the Tuskegee Airfield. *Courtesy Faith Serafin.*

Inside the hangar of the Tuskegee Airfield. *Courtesy Faith Serafin.*

in 1941, was actually designed by an African American architect. Training began in November of that year, before war had even commenced in America. Even though Pearl Harbor would not occur until a month later, leaders in Washington were beginning to feel the winds of war, and they wanted to be prepared for whatever the future might bring. By the end of 1943, the airfield had expanded to four runways and more than two hundred buildings, with 3,500 personnel on staff.

In the first class trained at the field, only five African American pilots made the cut. By the end of the war, nearly one thousand would follow in their footsteps. Sixty-six of these pilots were killed in action. Astonishingly, even more—eighty-four—were killed in training accidents. And it is these young men, those who never made it to combat but nevertheless lost their lives, who still haunt the old airfield in Tuskegee. At night, when the moon is new and the stars hide, a sound echoes through the forests that have now grown up where the airfield once stood. It is the sound of death, the screams of agony from the dying, the cries of those who see their fate approaching them. It is a haunting and a haunted place, one that is best to be avoided.

And there's another reason to avoid this place. It is now owned by a hunting club, one that values its exclusivity. The sign that hangs from the fence that surrounds the property reads, "WARNING! NO TRESPASSING!!! Anyone found here at night will be found here in the morning."

In other words, unless you want to join the spirits that haunt the airfield, it might be best to stay away.

Holt Cemetery

Why the dead would haunt the living is a mystery, but usually the reason for the location of a haunting is not. A house, a school, a battlefield…these are places where the best and worst moments of life may occur, places that are seared with the fires of life's most important events. But why would a ghost haunt a cemetery?

It might seem a strange question, particularly given the nervous feeling many of us get when walking past the gates of a city of the dead, especially when the sun has already set in the west. But whatever the case, some cemeteries seem as though they are more thoroughly infested with the spirits of the dead than others. Holt Cemetery on Society Hill is one of those places.

Holt Cemetery. *Photo by David Higdon.*

The interesting thing about Holt Cemetery is that the haunting is a public affair, not limited to the caretakers or people who live in the area. Visit Society Hill, and it is almost certain that you will hear the disembodied whispers of the past. Take a picture, and more often than not, something strange and uncanny will appear in the frame. Get a tape recorder and leave it running. When you play it back, you'll hear singing echoing back across time.

Where do these voices come from? What do they signify? To whom do they belong? It's likely we'll never know, and the spirits of Holt Cemetery will go on, never quite getting the rest they deserve.

Tuskegee National Forest

If you were only judging it by its size, you might not think much of the Tuskegee National Forest. It is the smallest national forest in the United States and resides entirely in Macon County. And yet the stories that are told about Tuskegee rival anything you've heard about the darkest and wildest forests.

Legends, myths and tales abound about the goings-on in Tuskegee. Witnesses have reported hearing strange noises from deep within the forest, and others have claimed to see flickering lights floating through the trees, like the flames of torches caught in the wind.

If local legend is to be believed, these phenomena originate from a time not all that long ago, when a new fear of devil worship was sweeping the nation. Largely discredited now, during this period, many experts feared that the youth of America were under the sway of dangerous new cults, specifically those that bowed their knees to Satan. And according to those who frequent Tuskegee, the small forest just east of Montgomery was the heart of these happenings.

It is said that these satanic cults would meet in the heart of the forest to commune with their dark gods. Before long, law enforcement became involved, and members of the Macon County Sheriff's Department conducted a raid of an old house deep within the woodlands. There they discovered the victims of horrific sacrifices. So incensed were they at what they saw that they burned the house to the ground, killing some of the cultists in the process. But they never did find the secret burial ground that was the devil worshipers' most sacred site. To this day, if you go out in the forest on dark nights lit only by the full moon, you will see the spirits of those long dead, as they haunt the cursed forest where they lost their lives.

Front sign of the Tuskegee National Forest. *Courtesy Faith Serafin.*

But it's not just ghosts you are liable to encounter in the forests of Tuskegee. One of the most famous stories to emerge from the forest happened only a few years ago. A couple was driving through the woods when the woman who was driving glanced into the brush along the road. There, she thought she saw the figure of someone crouching down, watching as the cars passed by. It was when the thing locked eyes with her that she realized it was not human.

The woman described the beast as having the basic shape of a man but covered in light-red hair from head to toe. For a long moment as the car crawled by, they looked at each other, before the figure took several big strides and disappeared into the forest. The woman almost wrecked her car while she was watching it move.

That's right. Alabama has Bigfoot sightings too.

PIKE COUNTY

Pike County is named for General Zebulon Pike (he of the noted peak). Troy is both the county seat and the largest city in Pike County. An up-and-coming city with a number of major industries in the area, Troy is also home to a university of the same name. But it is at a place called the Old Barfoot House that we will spend our time in Pike County.

Old Barfoot House

From the outside, there doesn't seem to be anything all that special about the place known as the Old Barfoot House. And, indeed, a talk with the owners of this private residence will reveal that nothing altogether unusual goes on there. At least, not these days. The same could not have been said during a period of five years from 1932 to 1937, when a dreadful poltergeist tormented the family who owned the home, finally driving them out, never to return.

It began one particularly bleak evening, when the children were tucked into bed and only the parents remained awake, sitting in their living room, enjoying the company of each other. Suddenly, they were not alone. As if out of nowhere, a man suddenly appeared. His hair was as black as the pants he wore, while his white shirt seemed to glow in the unnatural night. His eyes pierced into their souls, and the raging fire that burned there bespoke anger and hate. But it was the blood that flowed from his shoulders down to his waist, spilling off his legs and onto the floor, that terrified the poor young couple. They watched as the man turned, walking from the living room to the dining room, leaving puddles of blood behind as he went. It was only when they realized that he was heading to the back bedrooms, where their children slept, that they gave chase. The blood led all the way to the sleeping children's door, but when they burst into the room, no one was there.

Whatever small comfort they took from that was short-lived at best. The apparition continued to haunt them, and every day, the family grew more convinced that it was only a matter of time before he did them real harm. They held on for five years, but by then, they'd had enough, leaving forever. And with them went the spirit, never to be seen again.

If why the ghost came and where he went are complete mysteries, at least the history of the house lends some clue. Some thirty years earlier, in the late 1800s, a violent and inexplicable crime spree swept through Troy. Twenty-one men, women and children were found hacked to death by an axe, their bodies spread all over town. The frightened townspeople began to wonder if the murders and deaths would ever end, and they began looking for someone to blame. Suspicion soon fell on Tom Johnson, a local drifter in town who was considered a good-for-nothing. Fear and a desire for revenge won out over a sense of due process. On March 31, 1899, Tom Johnson was hanged from a gallows erected in the front yard of the Barfoot House.

Was Tom guilty? No one knows for certain, but it cannot be doubted that the murders ended with his life. Responsible or not, it certainly seems like Tom Johnson was the sort to haunt the Barfoot House—either as the spirit of an evil murderer or as the ghost of a man condemned to die for crimes he did not commit.

Russell County

Like so many of the counties in Alabama, Russell is named after a hero of the Creek Indian Wars, Colonel Gilbert C. Russell. Russell is most notable, however, for the bizarre history of its county seat, Phenix City. The last battle of the Civil War took place in Phenix City, but it wasn't until the 1940s that the town became famous around the country. They called it "Sin City," and for good reason.

Situated just across the border from Fort Benning, Georgia, it quickly became clear to the less savory elements of the city that there was money to be made from the young soldiers who often came through the town. Soon, the Phenix City Machine was born.

The Machine put some Mafia families to shame. Taking complete control of the city, Machine operatives opened bordellos and underground casinos and ran the liquor that supplied them all. For more than a decade, the good citizens of Phenix City lived in fear, and no one seemed willing to stand up to the Machine. But then came Albert Patterson.

Patterson was a local attorney from Russell County. He saw the corruption and crime that it bred firsthand, and he decided to take action. In 1954, he sought the Democratic nomination for attorney general of the State of Alabama on a platform of cleaning up Phenix City. In the runoff with Lee Porter of Gadsden, the Phenix City Machine went into action, begging, buying and stealing every vote it could get. It wasn't enough, and Patterson won the nomination. In 1954 Alabama, the general election result was a foregone conclusion. Patterson would be attorney general, and the Machine couldn't have that.

On the evening of June 18, 1954, Patterson remarked to a friend that he had a one in one hundred chance of ever being sworn in as attorney general.

He was right. That very night, an assassin shot him three times in the head as he walked to his parked car. He was dead before he hit the ground, but the Machine had finally gone too far.

Patterson accomplished with his death what the Machine had killed him to prevent him from doing in life. The governor of Alabama, Gordon Persons, decided that Phenix City was in a state of chaos and declared martial law in the city. The National Guard marched into town and deposed both the police department and the judiciary. Special prosecutors were deployed from Montgomery. It took six months, but the Machine was finally broken. An astonishing 734 indictments were issued against local law enforcement officers, elected officials and local business owners connected to organized crime. Three of those officials were indicted specifically for the murder of Patterson—Chief Deputy Sheriff Albert Fuller, Circuit Solicitor Arch Ferrell and Attorney General Si Garrett.

Today, you would never know that Phenix City had such an interesting and violent history. In fact, it was recently named the nation's No. 1 Best Affordable Suburb to raise a family. My, how things change.

Elite Café

The Elite Café has one real claim to fame: it was here that Albert Patterson was gunned down, in an alleyway just beside the café and the local police station. And there are some who say that Patterson's spirit remains where his life ended.

More than once, the local police have been called by panicked witnesses, sure that there is a man dying in the street next to the Elite. They describe a man who appears to have been shot, with blood pouring from his wounds. Each time, police vehicles speed to the scene, only to find nothing. No man, no bullet casings, no blood and no sign of any crime. At first, the angry police assumed that someone was playing a bad joke on them. Now it's happened so often that they just shrug their shoulders and go home.

Others have claimed to see a man walking in the alleyways of Phenix City. He is dressed in an outfit from decades before. But he never talks to anyone, and if you try and approach him, he simply disappears. Is this the ghost of Albert Patterson? Is he looking for those who killed him, still working to clean up a town that has been clean for more than fifty years? Or maybe he just wants to make sure that he's never forgotten.

Front view of Elite Café, where Albert Patterson died. *Courtesy Faith Serafin.*

Fort Mitchell Historic Site

Fort Mitchell is Alabama history. Built on a hill overlooking the Chattahoochee River, Fort Mitchell was constructed by the Georgia Militia as a stockade and base of operations during the Creek War of 1813. It was from this fort that American forces launched attacks against the Red Stick Indians. Once the Native Americans were subdued, Fort Mitchell took on a different role: shepherding the thousands of Indians who were forced to walk the Trail of Tears. When the Civil War came, Fort Mitchell passed into the hands of the Confederacy, and the men from Russell County who would go on to fight around the country were mustered at the fort.

Today, Fort Mitchell is a museum, reminding the people of Russell County of its role throughout the history of the state and the nation. But if the local residents are to be believed, it doesn't take much to remind them of the past. When the sun goes down, you are liable to run directly into it.

They say that spirits walk the streets of Fort Mitchell and that at night, you'll see a person who seems to be from another era or spirits that flash into being only to disappear. Whispers float on the wind, and

The Fort Mitchell Park cemetery. *Courtesy Faith Serafin.*

Fort Mitchell Park. *Courtesy Faith Serafin.*

voices call from another time. Some places are just more connected to the supernatural than others, and Fort Mitchell sure seems to be one.

Even Bigfoot has made an appearance in the area. In 2000, a terrified couple stumbled into a Quick Stop just down from Fort Mitchell, screaming for the attendant to call the police. The story they told was beyond belief. According to the man, the two had been camping when their dog, a yellow lab, started yelping. He went to check on the dog, and when he did, he ran straight into a beast that was eight feet tall and covered in fur. He wasted no time, emptying a clip from the pistol he carried with him into the beast, but it was unaffected by the shots. That's when they ran.

The two waited at the store until the police came. They had left everything at the site—dog, camping gear, everything. When the police arrived at the campsite, they found the equipment in relatively good order. The dog, however, was gone. Did these two see Bigfoot? Or were they indulging in more than hotdogs and s'mores at their campsite? It's hard to say, but one thing no one disagrees on is the fact that there are strange things that happen in Fort Mitchell. Strange things indeed.

TALLAPOOSA COUNTY

Tallapoosa County is probably known best for the quirky bend in the river that lends the county its name. They call it Horseshoe Bend. In many ways, it was at this place that the future of the United States was decided.

While it may seem like a foregone conclusion now that the loose series of battles that composed the Indian Wars and were spread over three centuries would end in a victory for the United States army, it was not always so clear. The definitive battle in that war occurred on March 27, 1814. The road to that engagement had started years before, when the great Indian war chief Tecumseh visited the Muscogee tribe, known to the Americans as the Creeks. To them, he delivered a speech filled with war and dreams of reconquest of long-lost lands (here found in Mike Bunn and Clay Williams's *Battle for the Southern Frontier*):

> *Oh! Muscogees, brethren of my mother, brush from your eyelids the sleep of slavery; once more strike for vengeance; once more for your country. The spirits of the mighty dead complain. Their tears drop from the weeping skies. Let the white race perish. They seize your land; they corrupt your women; they trample*

> *on the ashes of your dead! Back, whence they came, upon a trail of blood, they must be driven. Back! Back, ay, into the great water whose accursed waves brought them to our shores! Burn their dwellings! Destroy their stock! Slay their wives and children! The Red Man owns the country, and the Pale-faces must never enjoy it. War now! War forever! War upon the living! War upon the dead!*

When the war between the United States and Great Britain began in 1812, Tecumseh had his opportunity. At first, the war went Tecumseh's way. In the Battle of Detroit, Tecumseh and his forces joined with British redcoats to capture the city and the fort. It was said that the mere sight of Tecumseh's braves was so frightening that the Americans surrendered the city for fear a massacre would result. Detroit was a huge victory for the British, and had it not been for Commodore Perry's victory on the Great Lakes a year later, it might have spelled doom for the young country. Tecumseh's success was short-lived, though, and in the Battle of the Thames, the great Indian chief was killed. In the South, though, his spirit of rebellion lived on.

In the late summer of 1813, a band of Red Stick Creeks struck one of the worst blows the United States would suffer in the Indian Wars. One thousand Creek warriors descended on Fort Mims, near present-day Mobile, Alabama. After a battle that lasted the better part of the day, the Creek warriors captured the fort, killing or capturing five hundred men, women and children. Then they burned the fort to the ground.

Panic spread throughout the Southeast. Settlements were abandoned, with colonists fleeing west before the wrath of the Red Sticks. But then came a little-known politician and solider from Tennessee named Andrew Jackson. Jackson raised an army of more than three thousand men, including five hundred Cherokee and one hundred Lower Creek warriors who opposed the Red Sticks. The army advanced to the bend in the Tallapoosa River, where the Creeks had built a fortified position. There, one thousand Creek warriors waited to do battle with the whites, but it would be their brethren who would be their ultimate undoing.

While Jackson's army bombarded the Red Stick fortifications, his Cherokee and Creek allies swam across the river, attacking their enemies from the rear. Surrounded and vastly outnumbered, the Creek army was crushed, with eight hundred warriors dead. It was the greatest loss of life in any single battle of the Indian Wars. The Creeks were defeated. A few months later, Creek chieftains would cede the rest of their land to Andrew Jackson—much of which would become the state of Alabama—and a few years after that, he would be president.

Tallassee Community Library

Tallassee is one of those cities out of a dream, or perhaps a movie. It is an old city, filled with secrets and lore. Its downtown has seen better days, and yet one can feel the past surrounding you when you walk its streets. But the spirits of the dead seem closest in a place you would not expect: the Tallassee Library.

The Tallassee Library is, at first blush, nothing altogether special. A rather ordinary library building constructed in 1921, the little operation began with fewer than two thousand books. Today, it is a full-service library with twenty-six thousand books, seven computers and an annual circulation of thirty-four thousand. It is a hub of community activity in the little town of Tallassee, apparently for the living and the dead. You see, it's not so much what you *see* when you visit the Tallassee Library. It is what lies beneath. The property on which the building was constructed has an interesting history indeed.

If one travels down into the basement of the Tallassee Library, he or she will come to a large wooden door. Behind that door are the books the library keeps in storage. And from that room, one can enter another, smaller space. Here the foundations lie, not of the library, but of the building that came before—a small brick structure that served its purpose more than 150 years ago, when it was a Civil War hospital.

How many men died here? How many more were forever maimed and disfigured? History does not tell us. Nor would such figures account for the sheer number of hauntings reported at the Tallassee Library. Of all the locations contained in this book, Tallassee may very well be the most haunted.

It has gotten to the point that the library itself has started to keep a record of every paranormal event that has occurred in the building. Many of these events involve children. There once was a young father who had gone to the library with his wife and daughter. While he was standing among the stacks, he felt his little girl grab his hand. He turned to smile down at here, and no one was there. In fact, the daughter and mother had already gone home. Another time, a young boy entered the library and ran to the play area that the librarians keep for the small children. As he raced up the steps, he suddenly stopped. His mother asked what was wrong, to which the boy replied that he didn't want to play on the stage because he didn't know the two boys who were already up there. The mother followed the finger of her son as he pointed at the two strangers, but there was no one on the stage but him.

More than once, parents who are visiting the library have left their children in the play area. And more than once, those children have been witnessed seemingly playing catch with an invisible entity. In one particularly chilling instance, a little girl was playing with a small ball. A librarian watched as she looked up, smiled at the empty air and rolled the ball. The ball rolled for a few feet and then stopped suddenly. "Now roll it back," she said. To the utter astonishment of the witness, the ball, with no one anywhere near it, rolled gently back to the girl.

And it is not just the children who see spirits at the library. One of the librarians has personally witnessed a teenage boy holding the hand of a little girl. The two children walked into the stacks where the children's books are kept and then simply vanished. At least two customers have seen a young man, perhaps twenty or twenty-five, standing in the library, clothed in the fashions of the early 1900s. He removes one book after another, leafing through their pages, before returning them to the shelf. If one tries to speak with him, he ignores them, and if one approaches him, he simply disappears.

Kids' play area at the library. *Photo by David Higdon.*

Front view of the Tallassee Library. *Courtesy Faith Serafin.*

Yes, strange things happen at the Tallassee Library. A rocking horse tends to start rocking on its own. Patrons who are lost in a book have been known to feel their hair stroked by unknown hands. No one ever feels alone in the library, and more than one visitor has heard footsteps and felt hot breath on his or her neck, only to turn to an empty aisle.

Other events seem to be of the mischievous sort. Books are flipped upside down in the stacks. Pages turn on their own. Books are knocked off their shelves. Children can be heard laughing and running, but the rooms in which they should be are always empty upon inspection.

There are sounds so common that they have become almost part of the ordinary course of business in the library. People have reported hearing voices crying for help, others saying hello, some that are concerned with who these strangers are in their midst and others that ask them where visitors are going when they try and leave.

But perhaps the most interesting auditory phenomenon involves that of the piano. One late night, the librarian was at her desk when she started unconsciously humming along to the tune being played on a piano on the library. This continued for several minutes until she realized what she was doing. A cold wave passed over her as she realized not only that was she was alone but also that the library did not even own a piano.

How to explain all of this paranormal activity? Is the library built on a cemetery? Did something terrible happen there some time long ago? Or do ghosts just like to read? It's a mystery that is as inexplicable as the goings-on within the library at Tallassee.

Part II
Central Black Belt

Butler County

While no one knows precisely when Captain William Butler was born, the circumstances of his death are legendary. A native Virginian, Butler left the state of Georgia—where he had made his home and held elective office—to settle the wild territory of Alabama. When the Creek War began in 1813, Butler signed up. Within a year, victory was largely in hand for the settlers, but roving bands of hostile natives remained. On March 20, 1818, Butler was scouting a spring with a handful of other settlers. Native American troops under the command of an Indian war captain known only as Savannah Jack ambushed Butler. In the confusion, he and five other men disappeared. Their bodies were found the next day, badly mutilated. The spring quickly came to bear his name, and soon, so did the county.

Hank Williams was born within the confines of the county's borders. Some say that he never really left. Maybe it's his songs and the way they seem to echo a longing and desperation that goes beyond this world. Maybe it is his untimely death at the age of only twenty-nine. Maybe it is his eyes, bottomless pits that call out across the decades. But whatever the case may be, no one seems to want to let the ghost of Hank Williams rest.

Songs about ghosts are not rare in country music, but with Hank Williams, it seems as though they are a genre unto themselves. Whether he's picking up a hitchhiker in a phantom Cadillac in David Allen Coe's

"The Ride" or haunting the steps of Alan Jackson in "Midnight in Montgomery," Hank Williams seems to be truly immortal. And so do some of the spirits that still linger in Butler County.

Consolation Church

They say she comes at evening. When the moon dies and the night is black, she rises from the swamps and the forest that surround Consolation Church. Perhaps she comes as an old hag, bent and crooked. Other times, she is a beautiful girl, young and full of life. But it is her wail that all fear, the keen of one in mourning. Not for one dead. No, that would be too simple. She moans for one yet to die, for he who hears the cry of the banshee is doomed to not walk this earth for long.

She does not come alone. Red eyes haunt the tree-rimmed edge of the field in which sits the church. Demon howls rise from just beyond sight, and hellhounds walk about the cemetery on once hallowed ground, seeking those they will devour next. And then there are the children: a boy and a girl, neither of whom seem to notice the evil and frightening spirits that wheel about them. The boy plays with a ball. The girl skips along the road that leads to the place of worship. Neither speaks, although on occasion the sound of their laughter can be heard. If you see them, it's best you do not tarry long. And whatever you do, don't play ball with the boy. It is said that if he throws the ball to you, then you are as dead as if the banshee herself marked you for the grave.

These are the legends that stick like glue to Consolation Church, a small house of worship on the Butler and Covington County lines. In addition to banshees and hellhounds and demon children, there are tales of Confederate soldiers who still march to battle and even an outhouse that traps the user inside its flimsy wooden walls.

How much of this is true? How much of it is legend, urban or otherwise? Who can say? And even if it's not true, who wants to believe that, anyway?

CONECUH COUNTY

Death has seemingly hung around Conecuh County ever since an incident from the late 1700s led to a river in the region receiving the moniker of "Murder Creek." The story goes that a party of half a dozen men led by Colonel Joseph Kirkland stopped for the night on the banks of the creek and were ambushed by three fugitives from the law. The three men killed the men while they slept, stealing the money that they carried with them for the journey. A posse was formed, and the leader of the fugitives was captured. In way of justice, the man was taken to the very spot where the crime had been committed—it was said that the trees were still wet with the blood of the innocent slain—and there he was executed.

Is the story true? Who can really say, but whatever the case, Conecuh County has come to be famous for more than just the sausage that bears its name, for the nights in the area are rarely silent, and the place is thick with stories of the supernatural and undead.

Old Carter Hospital

Carter Hospital in the little town of Repton may not look like much—you'd probably mistake it for an old house—but for decades it was the only hospital from Selma to Pensacola, Florida. To the people who came

Front hallway of Old Carter Hospital in Repton. *Courtesy Lee Peacock.*

there with emergencies, just barely clinging to life, it must have appeared to be a godsend. Harper Lee had her appendix removed at Old Carter, and hundreds of others had lifesaving surgery performed there. It was only when a federal law was passed that provided money for every county to open a hospital that Old Carter faded into obscurity. It is said that the very day that a hospital opened in the neighboring county, the doctor who ran Old Carter locked the door and walked out. That was in the '50s. The building has stood silent since then—at least, for the most part.

Like any hospital, it cannot be doubted that hundreds of the souls who entered through Carter's doors never left alive. They say that the dead walk the halls at night and that a feeling of unease hangs over the rooms. There's still blood on the ceiling from past surgeries, and sometimes, even though the building has been shut up for decades, the smell of antiseptic and sterile bandages wafts along on the breeze. Lights dance through the empty recovery rooms, and the door to the downstairs basement is known to open and close on its own. Old Carter may have been long closed, but for the dead, it is still open for business.

Castleberry Bank Building

The old Castleberry Bank Building has seen better days. From the boarded-up windows covering smashed panes to the ramshackle siding that's rapidly falling into disrepair, you'd never know that it once held the busy financial center of town, as well as the city post office. Tiny Castleberry—also known as the "strawberry capital of Alabama"—is the kind of place where everybody knows everything about everybody else, and the haunting of Castleberry Bank is a popular story.

It seems that before the Great Depression, the president of the bank was one of the richest men in town, and his wealth only grew in size as the Roaring Twenties roared on. But what he couldn't know has now become history. The stock market crashed, and the bank's finances collapsed. The president lost everything. Perhaps it's not surprising that one day, he went into his office, closed the door behind him and put a gun in his mouth. And from that moment, the old bank at Castleberry was haunted.

It is a bizarre and disturbing haunting, too. There are the ordinary manifestations of a spirit one might expect, all disturbing in their own right. They say that cigar smoke wafts through the building, even though no one has smoked a cigar there in decades. The voice of a man echoes through its halls, even when no man is present. Objects move during the night or disappear altogether for no reason whatsoever.

But it is something else that chills the blood and bones of those who go within the old Castleberry bank. Nothing lives inside the bank. Even though the breeze blows through open windows and broken doors, there are no insects, no mice, no creatures within. It is as if they fear the place instinctively. But it's not just life that flees this place. It is sound as well. Nothing stirs inside. A heavy feeling weighs on the shoulders of all who enter. The building does not settle. The doors do not creak. The passing of cars is not heard. The only sound is the footsteps of unknown spirits and the voices of ghostly men.

Castleberry Bank safe. *Courtesy Lee Peacock.*

CRENSHAW COUNTY

Crenshaw County is the kind of place where you might drive through it and never see another soul. With a population of under fourteen thousand people—that's only twenty-two people per square mile—everyone in the county named after Judge Anderson Crenshaw knows everybody else. And something else they know is the story of the Mary Daniel Bridge.

Mary Daniel Bridge

In Crenshaw County, they say that if you want to have a real paranormal experience, you need only to go to the Mary Daniel Bridge. It happened in the late 1800s or early 1900s, depending on who is telling the story at the time. Mary Daniel was somewhat infamous in the county as being one who walked with the devil in the dark watches of the night. In other words, she was a witch.

According to old legends, witches had particular difficulty in passing running streams of water. And perhaps that explains what happened to Mary Daniel on the bridge that now unofficially bears her name. The story goes that she and her baby (a daughter) were crossing the bridge when an accident befell them. What exactly it was remains unclear. Perhaps the horses were spooked. Perhaps Mary was just a poor driver. But whatever the case, mother and baby went off of the bridge and plunged into the river below. The baby drowned, sadly. They buried her not one hundred yards from the bridge in a small cemetery. The tragedy, however, had not ended. Mary's husband, drunk with anger and driven insane by despair, dragged her to the bridge where his daughter lost her life. And there he hanged her before throwing himself to his death. No one knows where Mary's body was buried, but it wasn't long before Mary's spirit returned.

The Mary Daniel Bridge is a truly spooky location. They say that if you come to the bridge at night, you'll see the disembodied spirit of Mary walking the road, calling for her lost child. And even if you don't see her, you feel her. There have also been reports of strange orbs of light that float along the river below, occasionally rising to greet visitors to the bridge.

But it's not just the bridge itself that is haunted. The graveyard that lies less than a football field away is also purportedly the home of ghosts. Mary is seen there as well, as if she knows that her daughter is buried within its confines somewhere. And it is not just her spirit that is present. Mary, after all, was thought to be a witch, and many have reported encountering "night watchers," dark entities left by Mary to guard the cemetery where her daughter was buried. It is said that anyone who enters the cemetery at night invites a curse and even death.

That curse came true at a site up the road, where a half-built house stands. According to local lore, the house was under construction when the workers began to flee in droves, with some of them being injured by invisible forces. Soon, no one would dare to enter the property, and the half-constructed house remains to this day.

Is the Mary Daniel Bridge haunted? The locals certainly think so, and given the feeling you get during a visit, it's almost impossible to argue with them.

Dallas County

Dallas County is as thick with history as the air is itself on a hot, muggy night in downtown Selma. It was here in a place called Old Cahawba that Alabama had its first state capital in a once thriving city that is now an empty ghost town. It is here where great battles of the civil rights era were fought and won. And it is here where a young southern belle by the name of Kathryn Tucker Windham first met a ghost she called Jeffrey, sparking a love for the paranormal that would inspire her to become one of the great storytellers of this or any age. Yes, to walk through Dallas County is to walk through history. Sometimes, if you listen real close, that history begins to speak through the voices of those long dead.

Old Cahawba

In the oldest days of Alabama, when the state was little more than a territory and the stories of Indian wars still carried the air of reality, Old Cahawba was a booming city with nothing but glory before it. In 1820, it became the capital of the state, and everyone had all the reason to assume that it would remain so.

But Cahawba had its enemies. A state capital means money, and it means power. There were those in other areas of the state who craved both, and they began to plot the city's downfall. Cahawba's relatively low elevation proved to be the key to their efforts. Cahawba, not unlike many places along the river, suffered the occasional flood. Some started to whisper that the air around Cahawba was spoiled and that the rising waters rendered the area unsuitable for a capital. Only six years after it became the center of state government in Alabama, Cahawba watched as that distinction slipped away. Soon after, it was almost deserted.

But Cahawba refused to die. In truth, the flooding problems at Cahawba were no worse than at any another town that could boast a connection to the river. Before long, people—and businesses—returned to Cahawba, and it became a major shipping port for cotton coming from the other Black Belt counties down the Alabama River to Mobile. Once the railroad came through in 1859, it seemed as though Cahawba was back for good. But then came the Civil War, which would destroy Cahawba just as it would destroy most of the South.

First, the rail line was ripped up and moved to another, more important destination for the Confederate army. Then, a Union prison was placed

Old Cahawba (floating light location "orb" site). *Courtesy Faith Serafin.*

at the heart of the city. And just as the war ended, the biggest flood in its history struck Cahawba. By the turn of the century, nothing much walked the streets of Cahawba but the occasional coyote—nothing much alive, that is.

Cahawba had become a ghost town, and not in name only. And the ghost that haunts Cahawba even has a name. They call it "Pegues's Ghost." Now, Pegues is not the name of the ghost itself, but rather one of Cahawba's leading lights, Colonel C.C. Pegues. They say that it was first seen by a young couple, stealing away behind the colonel's home, running through the garden maze of the house. The two young lovers were shadowed by a glowing light. No doubt, at first they worried that it was the lantern of an angry chaperone. But this light acted funny. Sometimes it would be ahead of them, sometimes behind. Sometimes it would be to the side and occasionally above. And when they got close, until they could almost touch it, it would simply vanish away, only to appear later. At first, they called it a will-o'-the-wisp, but then it just became Pegues's Ghost.

Why did it come? Perhaps it was a warning to Colonel Pegues himself, who would die that same year. Or maybe to the town of Cahawba, a city that would soon vanish into the wilderness, just like the ghost was said to do.

Front view of the Old Cahawba (Kirkpatrick home). *Courtesy Faith Serafin.*

But even though the maze is gone, and even though the home and the town have fallen away, the flame of Pegues remains. And if you go into the forest and make your way to the old road that leads to the dead town in the heart of Alabama, you just might find a fiery visitor shadowing your every step.

Vaughan-Smitherman Museum

The Vaughan-Smitherman Museum has a long and venerated history. It was built in 1847 by the Selma Freemasons as a school for orphans and children of their indigent brothers. It functioned as a school for a while, but the necessities of war pressed on it, and it became a Confederate hospital. Circumstances flipped in the years following the war, and it was converted into Selma's first hospital for the treatment of African Americans. It then went on to serve as a temporary location for the Dallas County Courthouse before becoming a military academy. It then returned to its medical roots—housing the Vaughan Memorial Hospital—before finally becoming a museum depicting Selma's rich and diverse history.

Front view of the Vaughan-Smitherman Museum. *Courtesy Faith Serafin.*

And given the museum's own history, it's no surprise that it comes with spiritual baggage. Several events mark this spectral presence. Footsteps coming down the stairs and echoing along the hardwood floor, toilets that flush on their own and elevators that run up and down without anyone inside. There's also a picture of William Rufus King, the founder of Selma, a United States senator and even a vice president of the United States. It's been said that King's spirit is ever-present within the building. One member of the museum staff made the mistake of uttering a disparaging remark about King one night. A lamp sitting underneath the picture of the former vice president rose in the air and then slammed down onto the desk on which it sits. Respect for the dead, it seems, is a required trait for anyone who would spend time in the Vaughan-Smitherman Museum.

Tally Ho Restaurant

The Tally Ho restaurant is the kind of place that's just sort of always been there. One of Selma's landmarks, the Tally Ho has been around for at least eighty years, but probably even longer than that. By the 1930s, the owners of the restaurant had found a more lucrative occupation—gambling and prostitution. Many of the wealthiest citizens in Selma and Montgomery would find their way to the Tally Ho for a game or two, or maybe something a little more. That continued until the federal authorities got wind of these "activities," and the Tally Ho had to abandon its operations. And so it turned to serving liquor instead. The officers at Craig Air Force Base got wind of the services that the Tally Ho offered and turned the place into an unofficial club. The owners of the restaurant knew a good thing when they saw it, and for twenty-five dollars, they gave not only entrance to the club but also a mug with the member's name that remained permanently at the store.

The restaurant remains in Selma, having expanded significantly and, in true Tally Ho fashion, installed the marble flooring from the original state capital in the town of Cahawba.

A place like the Tally Ho would not be complete without a ghost. They call her Betty, and common knowledge declares that she was a bit of a party girl who frequented the restaurant during its days as a speakeasy. Betty was famous among the young men of the day for a powerful lilac perfume that she always wore. On more than one occasion, patrons or workers in the Tally Ho have reported smelling the sweet fragrance of lilacs even when there is seemingly no cause. Betty doesn't just make the place smell better,

Left: Interior view of the Tally Ho Restaurant. *Courtesy Faith Serafin.*

Below: Front view of the Tally Ho Restaurant. *Courtesy Faith Serafin.*

though. She is also known for playing jokes at the Tally Ho. Sometimes the lights turn off and on without cause. Other times, the chandelier in the main dining room will swing wildly, to the amazement of gathered guests.

Betty is a friendly ghost, though. She just wants to have a good time, and she picked the perfect place to do it.

Old Depot Museum

To step into the Old Depot Museum is to step into history, in more ways than one. Back before it became attached to the moniker "old," the depot served as the Selma railway stop for the Louisville & Nashville Railway, whose service boomed in the years following the Civil War. Today, the Old Depot is a museum dedicated to the history of the Black Belt. Its exhibits span from the antebellum days of the region all the way to the present age. They also include one restless spirit that likes to ride the elevator.

There's a reason for that. When the elevator for the museum was constructed, the workers had to dig down into the earth below the depot. And when they did, they hit ruins that were part of the old arsenal and artisan well that was once of critical importance to the Southern war effort.

Front view of the Old Depot Museum. *Courtesy Faith Serafin.*

Thousands were employed at the arsenal, and Nathan Bedford Forrest had committed to protecting the works there. In an effort to destroy this critical Southern industry, a battle was even fought in the Selma area. Many young men were killed, and much of Selma was burned to the ground.

With records from the time being what they are, who can say what young men died in the shadow of what is now the depot? Who can say what restless spirits might still haunt its grounds? All we can know for sure is that many have reported feeling a presence in the depot and that the elevator, the one that rests in that pit dug from the ruins of battles past, is its favorite abode.

Sturdivant Hall

There are many houses in this book that could be said to represent the style of the antebellum plantations. But without a doubt, none can lay claim to that title more firmly than Sturdivant Hall in Selma. Its white walls, massive Corinthian columns and beautiful cast-iron balcony are quintessential Old South.

Built in 1856 during the height of Southern wealth and power, its initial years were filled with instability and political intrigue. Edmund Watts, the man who built the house, lived in it with his family for only a few months before pulling up stakes and moving to Texas. He sold it to John McGee Parkman, a man who had all the looks of someone who was going to make it out of the Civil War a wealthy man. Parkman was from a good family, had an excellent education and had, from a very early age, shown an uncanny ability to master delicate financial matters. When the conflict ended, he became president of the most prominent bank in the area at the age of only twenty-nine. Unfortunately, he would last at that position for only three years. Under his leadership, the bank engaged heavily in cotton speculation. But with the war over, the price of cotton took a nosedive, and the bank lost extensively—including money given to it by the United States government for Reconstruction. The military governor of Alabama, Wager Swayne, arrested Parkman and had him imprisoned at Castle Morgan, the old Confederate prison for Union soldiers in Cahaba. Parkman made the ill-advised move to try and escape captivity. He was shot in the process.

The history of the house stabilized at this point, passing to the Gillman family, who owned it until the City of Selma purchased the estate with a gift

Front view of Sturdivant Hall. *Courtesy Faith Serafin.*

from Robert Daniel Sturdivant. But in at least one person's view, the house has always belonged to John McGee Parkman.

On the day he was arrested, Parkman swore an oath: he had not been responsible for the losses of the bank's funds, he was innocent and he would return to his home. If those who have lived and worked in the Sturdivant are correct, he kept that promise.

It started soon after his death. Many of his servants simply refused to enter certain rooms on the property, claiming that they were occupied by some unworldly creature. Visitors began to report cold drafts of wind on the warmest day, spots that stole every ounce of warmth from your body, leaving the victim pale and disoriented. Others have seen the shadowy figure of a man strolling through the halls of the mansion with an air of confidence that could only bespeak ownership of the place.

Has Parkman returned to his home, as he promised so long ago? Does he seek to prove his innocence and clear his name? Perhaps if you ever walk the halls of the Sturdivant and feel the ice-cold air pass through your soul, you can ask him.

Weaver Castle

Unlike so many of the grand homes in Selma, Weaver Castle is not an elegant, columned, antebellum masterpiece that looks like it came straight from *Gone with the Wind*. Rather, it is, as its name suggests, patterned after a Gothic castle built along the Rhine River in Germany. Designed and built by Lieutenant William Weaver of the Confederate army, Weaver Castle is perhaps most famous for being the childhood home of artist and Tiffany stained-glass designer Clara Weaver Parrish. So unique is the architectural design of the Weaver Castle that part of the structure is now in a Birmingham museum.

Weaver was built in 1868 by William M. Weaver, a landowner and husband of Lucretia Weaver. The Weavers lived happily in their home until their son suddenly fell ill. No one knew exactly what was wrong with the boy, but it was clear that if he didn't get some sort of help, he was not long for this world. Alas, the medical field was not then what it is now, and nothing could save the boy. His father followed swift on his heels, dead of a broken heart. The house has been haunted ever since.

An eerie phantom light floats through the hallway, and more than once, passersby have gone to warn the family who now live in the Weaver Castle

Front view of the Weaver Castle. *Courtesy Faith Serafin.*

that they left a light on in the attic. The only problem? There is no electricity in this upper floor and, thus, no light. None from this world, at least.

If it is the ghost of William Weaver haunting his old home, he is not quiet about his wishes. Music plays throughout the night, no matter that no one in the home is responsible. Once, the matron of the family who calls Weaver Castle home had a dog. The dog began to bark. Suddenly, a voice rang out, "Dog, shut up!" The dog quickly fell silent, but then it was the startled lady who was making noise. She was alone, and a futile search of every room in the house revealed no one from whom the voice could have come.

A workman in the house once experienced the wrath of the spirit as well. When he was installing an overhead ceiling fan, someone asked him what he was doing. The man answered, explaining that he had been hired to do some work around the home. The question was repeated, and the man, thinking that it was odd, turned around to speak to the man directly. The room was empty. He didn't wait to finish his installation before he fled the home.

Weaver Castle is an architectural oddity, and it is a spiritual one as well. Perhaps one day, William Weaver can come to terms with the death of his son and leave the good people who now call his old house their home well enough alone.

Brownstone Manor

"So we beat on, boats against the current, borne back ceaselessly into the past." So ends one of the most celebrated works of American fiction, *The Great Gatsby*. The past is all around us, and at Brownstone Manor in Selma, so, too, are memories of F. Scott Fitzgerald and his bride, Zelda. They came here often, and perhaps for an afternoon they forgot the troubles that haunted them both—alcohol for Fitzgerald and a creeping insanity for Zelda.

The gorgeous, colonnaded Brownstone Manor was built in 1898 by J.B. Ellis as the first modern mansion in Alabama. It came complete with central heating, central air, indoor plumbing and full electricity. Unfortunately, Mr. Ellis only lived in the house for a brief four months, the cost to construct it being too much for his limited funds. It was then bought by the Hoopers. Mrs. Hooper loved the house so much that she raised her six children in the guesthouse—they were not allowed in the main building until they were sixteen. When Mrs. Hooper died in 1953, her will instructed that she lie in repose for four days in the music room before having her funeral in the dining room. Some say she never quite left.

Front gate of the Brownstone Manor. *Courtesy Faith Serafin.*

Front view of the Brownstone Manor. *Courtesy Faith Serafin.*

You name it, and it has happened at the Brownstone. Pictures fall off the walls for no reason. The sound of high-heeled shoes clicking through the halls is a regular occurrence, even if the house is empty with the exception of the listener. The owners of the home feel Mrs. Hooper's friendly presence regularly, whether it is on the bed, in the room where she would often sit and enjoy the summer sunset or in the hallways. Never in the kitchen, though, for a southern lady of her stature would never have deigned to enter the kitchen—that was for the hired help.

Surely, the Brownstone remains Mrs. Hooper's. All the rest of us are only visitors.

St. James Hotel

Even though it is perhaps one of the most historic hotels in Alabama, the actual history of the St. James Hotel in Selma is hotly debated. Pretty much everyone agrees that it was built in 1831 and originally named the Brantley Hotel after Brigadier General John Brantley, the man who headed the stock consortium that financed its construction. Because it was built adjacent to the docks on the Alabama River, it was a hotspot and a hive of activity, one that provided lodging, meals and entertainment for the merchants who plied their wares up and down the river.

Despite its popularity, the hotel was constantly changing owners. Sometime before the Civil War, it fell to Dr. James Gee, who renamed it the Troupe House. Gee turned the property over to his slave, Benjamin Sterling Turner, who was lucky in that he had an education. He also demonstrated quite an aptitude for management. When the Civil War ended, Turner became the mayor of a rebuilding Selma and was the first African American to serve in the United States Congress.

During the Civil War, Selma was a major manufacturing center for the Confederacy, distributing supplies and weapons up and down the Alabama River. When the war turned irrevocably against the South, Selma became a target. Once the city fell in 1865, many of the buildings in the downtown area and particularly the port were burned to the ground. The hotel only survived because the Union troops had made it their base of operation.

But with the war over, Selma had a rebirth. Captain Tom Smith bought the hotel, giving it the name by which we now know it: the St. James. The hotel did well during this period. In 1885, a bridge across the Alabama River

Two bronze horses outside the St. James Hotel. *Courtesy Faith Serafin.*

was constructed just south of the hotel. While the original bridge is long gone, the bridge keeper's cottage still stands adjacent to the hotel.

As the decades passed, the hotel became more of a center for drinking and dancing than it did a place for overnight guests, with its guest rooms losing out in favor of newer and nicer hotels. Soon, it became more of a boardinghouse, but despite what might be thought of as a decline in its stature, it was then that the St. James experienced its most famous guests: the outlaws Jesse and Frank James.

It seems that Jesse James had a woman in Selma, one he was quite fond of. He'd visit her often in the St. James, and her portrait hangs in the hotel sitting room to this day.

In the 1890s, the St. James was closed as a hotel. It was used as a commercial office, a feed store and a mechanic shop. Still, the main building fared pretty well over the next one hundred years. Eventually, the City of Selma recognized its historical significance, purchasing it for the purpose of preserving the building. Today, those who visit the St. James find a modern hotel built within the bones of a historic boardinghouse. And while much has changed about the old hotel, some believe that one thing that remains the same is some of the guests who have decided never to check out.

Left: Bar area of the St. James Hotel. *Courtesy Faith Serafin.*

Below: Front view of the St. James Hotel. *Courtesy Faith Serafin.*

And that is why many people believe that the St. James Hotel is the most haunted place in all of Alabama. It's Jesse James, perhaps not surprisingly, who is most often reported to haunt the hotel that bears his name. They say that they see him sometimes, walking through the halls in the dress of the nineteenth-century, attire that befits his reputation as a lawless bandit. Others have seen him in rooms 214, 314 and 315, the rooms James most often inhabited. At other times, he is seen sitting at a table in the bar, perhaps watching the door lest he get shot in the back. At still other times, the smell of lavender seems to waft about the rooms, the same scent that his lover, Lucinda, was known to wear.

But it's not just the leader of the James-Younger Gang that visitors to the St. James have reported. In the courtyard, full cadres of spirits have been seen, all garbed in the dress of a grand ball. And weaving among all these spirits is a black dog, one that more than once has kept guests at the hotel awake with its nonstop barking. But when guests or staff investigate, no dog is ever found.

What brings these spirits to the St. James? Why don't they leave? It's impossible to say. Perhaps they just love the parties.

Baker House

From the outside, the Baker House looks to the world like a picture-perfect antebellum home. The Italianate-style house, draped in Spanish moss and surrounded by magnolia trees, is the image of the lost South. And it retains that part of history, in more ways than one.

George O. Baker, a coal magnate, built the house in 1858. He could not have imagined what it would see in only a few short years. As the Civil War drew to a close, the invading Union army met with Confederate troops outside of Selma. More than two dozen women and children fled to the Baker House seeking shelter. As the chaos of war exploded around them, two young men were brought into the house, both badly wounded. One was a Confederate and the other a Union soldier. But in that moment, it made no difference. Those in the house fought to save the lives of those two men. In the case of the Southerner, they succeeded. The boy in blue was not so fortunate. Despite their best efforts, he died there in the house, near the grand staircase.

Perhaps it is because he left this world in the home, or perhaps it is because his blood still stains the floor to this day, but most who have set foot in the

Front view of the Baker House. *Courtesy Faith Serafin.*

Baker House swear that they did not do so alone. They hear his footsteps in back rooms that should be empty. Dark shadows take human form and move across the wall. An overwhelming sense of sadness seems to dominate the place, while the creaking floors and opened doors portend a presence that is altogether unworldly.

Kenan's Mill

Kenan's Mill in Selma has been in operation long beyond the memory of the living. Dating to before the Civil War, the mill was an absolute necessity for a way of life that those of us in the twenty-first century can scarcely imagine. For more than one hundred years, until the 1960s, Kenan's Mill served the people of Selma who needed their corn ground into cornmeal and grits, two staples of most meals during that time. The mill served as a center for the social life of the folks who lived in the area as well. Dances were held there, a swimming area was maintained and it was not uncommon to see lovers enjoying a picnic in the shade of the old building.

At top speed, the mill could grind more than a ton of corn every day. Suspended over the rushing waters of the Valley Creek, the mill's power was provided by a turbine beneath its floor. The original millstones—more than four feet wide—are still in the mill to this day. Every year, the people of Selma come together to run the mill once again, reliving a traditional way of life that was simpler, if not easier.

The past calls out to you at Kenan's Mill. The sound of rushing water smashing against ancient stone speaks a language of its own, and as the sun sets over this idyllic spot, you never feel completely alone. Most of the stories in this book tell of lights and voices and things that go bump in the night. Very few of them involve actual physical manifestations of spirits, but Kenan's Mill is famous for just that sort of occurrence. They say that if you go inside the mill as dusk settles over the river, the spirits that remain in the place will come out to play. And it seems that tag is their preferred game. Visitors to the mill have reported having their clothes tugged on, being tapped on the shoulder, grabbed, pushed and even slapped. Some have reported seeing the spirit of an old man walking around the ruins—still others, the voice of a young boy or the distinctive sound of children's laughter.

Maybe it's just the sound of the bubbling brook or the late afternoon sun playing tricks on the eyes. And yet, how to explain the shoves and the physical interaction? Some things, it seems, really don't have logical explanations.

Purifoy-Lipscomb House

One of the oldest houses in the Furman, Alabama area, the Purifoy-Lipscomb House was built in 1840. Unlike many of the houses we visit, it actually stayed in the hands of its original owners—the Purifoy family—all the way until 1987, eventually passing to the Lipscombs.

In the 1870s, a major drought struck the area. While we can't imagine it now, at that time, there was no indoor plumbing, and there was no central water supply. If you couldn't get it from somewhere nearby, you went without. That meant no water for crops and no water for Dr. Purifoy's practice. The doctor had to do something, so he sent his servants to a spring a full half-mile away. But unfortunately, they never came back with any water. They did come back with stories though.

The local legends were thick around Furman, and many people believed that a witch haunted the spring and that no one could recover water from it successfully without her blessing. Apparently, Dr. Purifoy did not meet with her approval. Purifoy would not be deterred. He decided that he would dig a well, one deep enough that even the drought would not stop him from recovering the water he needed.

His servants weren't up to the task, so Purifoy hired some professional well diggers to do the tough and exhausting work. He bought lumber to case the well with, and down they started digging, reinforcing the well with the wooden boards as they went. Purifoy had been without water for a while, and he told the well diggers that he would pay them extra if they could finish quickly. This led them to make a very foolish decision.

The diggers soon discovered that they could make much faster progress if they didn't bother to encase the well with wood. Deeper and deeper they went. But then, after the sun had already fallen below the horizon, the sides of the well collapsed, trapping one of the diggers below. Dr. Purifoy heard the horrified shouts of his workers, and once he learned what had happened, he sent one of them into town to get help. As the night fell on the countryside, dozens of men came to Purifoy's aid.

They started digging, urged on by the pitiful cries of the man buried below. "Help me! Help me!" he cried, "Get me out of here!" Down and down they went, but not as fast as they would have liked. Another cave-in was always a threat, and even though the buried man implored them to hurry, they had to be careful.

For hours they dug, into the night, but no matter how far down they went, they could not find him. By the time the sun had risen again, the sounds of the man had stopped. The townspeople determined that it was too dangerous to try and recover the body. The man was never found.

The cries started almost immediately after, and they have continued to this day. At night, when the sun sets and the moon rises, pitiful shouts start to echo across the field surrounding the old Purifoy home. "Help me!" a voice cries. "Help me!" And if a soul is brave enough to continue on to the spot where the cursed well was meant to be dug, he'll see a shadowy figure hunched over the depression in the ground, weeping into his hands and wailing, "Get me out of here!"

LOWNDES COUNTY

Many of the counties in the Black Belt were instrumental in the fight for civil rights in Alabama and the nation, but few had as much to overcome as Lowndes County. Even in 1965, a century after the Civil War had finally come to a close, fewer than one hundred white families owned 80 percent of the land in the county. Meanwhile, not a single black resident was registered to vote, even though blacks constituted more than 75 percent of the population.

They called it "Bloody Lowndes." The name was well earned. Black citizens were kept in a position of subservience through violence and intimidation, and lynchings and beatings were not uncommon early on. But by 1965, the long-oppressed people of Lowndes County watched as marchers passed through their county on the way to Selma. It was during this march that Viola Liuzzo, a Michigan mother of five, was shot and killed by members of the Ku Klux Klan as she ferried civil rights workers through the county. Her death would not be in vain. Civil rights organizations moved in and fought back. A year later, more than half the registered voters in the country were African American. It was only a first step, but it was one that would eventually presage a new dawn of equality in the county, the state and the country.

And yet, like so many places with so much history, not all of it is fully in the past.

Marengo Manor

Marengo Manor is a house that moved—literally. Marengo was conceived by Dr. John Howard as a home for both his medical practice and his family. He built the house along the Alabama River, just north of Lowndesboro. It turned out to be a poor choice. With his medical practice suffering from a lack of patients, the good doctor decided to start over. But why build a new house when he already had one he loved? So, the doctor, being an enterprising man, had his slaves dismantle the house piece by piece. The pieces were then moved by barge across the river to the city proper.

Eventually, the house passed from one doctor to another when Dr. Charles Edwin Reese purchased it shortly before the Civil War. Reese is remembered fondly by the people of Lowndesboro for a ruse he pulled during the closing days of the Civil War that likely saved the city from destruction. Union troops advancing north after the Battle of Mobile were destroying anything that they determined could be used by Confederate forces for military purposes. In these calculations, they were liberal in their assessments. Thus, town after town was burned to the ground. As the army of General James T. Wilson came within sight of Lowndesboro, Dr. Reese went to the camp on a "humanitarian" mission. He told Wilson that the area was under quarantine and that smallpox ran rampant throughout the town. Wisely, Wilson decided that discretion was the better part of valor and spared the town.

By the 1920s, the house had passed into the ownership of L. James Powell, the man who first called it Marengo Manor. His son inherited the property in 1959, and it was during his ownership that the home turned from a place of happiness to one of foreboding. Powell was married, and while he loved his wife, Kathleen, very much, there was little he could do to alleviate her poor health. She was wheelchair-bound, and because she had great difficulty getting around, she was constantly afraid of being left alone. Powell was a businessman, though, and he could not be with his wife at all times. To make her feel better, he bought her a pistol and taught her how to use it. Very soon, she would.

One dark, southern Alabama night, Powell left Kathleen behind while he drove some overly intoxicated guests home from a party he had hosted at their home. When he returned, he found Kathleen dead. She had been shot once in the head, the bullet coming from her own gun. The police investigated, and despite James's protestations, they ruled the death a suicide. But how could it be? How could she have reached her gun, the one that she kept on the opposite side of the room? True, she could have used her crutches, but they were far from her bed and far from her reach. It didn't add up.

Was Kathleen murdered? It is impossible to say. But whether to tell the world the truth or because her soul regretted the choice to end her life, things weren't the same at Marengo Manor after her death. A deep sense of foreboding fell on the property. A cold, empty breeze blew through its corridors. Cackles of insane laughter echoed down its halls. For years, the house sat empty. When the new owners purchased the house, they decided to turn it into a restaurant. But a vengeful ghost was bad for business. The Dohertys, the new family, were desperate, so they turned to a psychic.

The psychic claimed that she made contact with the ghost, a woman who called herself Kathleen. The psychic reported that the woman understood that she was not wanted and that she would be gone by February—the month of Kathleen's birth and death. And when February came, the sense of foreboding seemed to lift from Marengo Manor.

And yet ghostly whispers can still be heard by those who live within the manor—that is, if their hearing is attuned to the world beyond. Many visitors to Marengo Manor claim to still see the spirit of a woman within its walls, particularly in the basement. Some claim it is Kathleen. Others say that this spirit is from a different period of the house's history, from when Dr. Howard still called the manor home. But whatever the case may be, one thing that cannot be denied is that Marengo Manor never sits empty.

MONROE COUNTY

They call the tiny southern county of Monroe, named after the fifth president of the United States, the literary capital of Alabama. Truman Capote called its county seat of Monroeville home, as did Nelle Harper Lee, author of the most famous book to ever come out of the state (and one of the best books ever written), *To Kill a Mockingbird.* Perhaps drawn by the literary flavor of the place, there are plenty of haunted locations in and around Monroeville and throughout the rest of the county.

Rikard's Mill Historical Park

Every October, when the days grow short and the winds blow cold, children and adults alike gather at Rikard's Mill Historical Park in Beatrice to listen to tales of spirits and spooks that haunt the surrounding area. Some folks think that the site is perfect for such tales, especially since it has one or two of its own to add to the list. Perched on the edge of the waters of Flat Creek, a tributary of the Alabama River, Rickard's Mill was built in 1845 by Jacob "Jake" Rikard. The mill still functions, and if visitors are so inclined, they can watch how corn and wheat were turned into the precious cornmeal and flour that farmers in small communities depended on to feed their family in days long gone by.

Rikard actually built the mill to supplement his income as a blacksmith, but at first, his plans didn't quite work out as he had hoped. A flood—always a danger with a business that uses the power of the water to run—destroyed the first mill, and the building that now sits in the state park is actually from the late 1860s.

But whatever remains of the physical building, the nonphysical is just as present. Many hauntings are, at their heart, a strange feeling, a sense that we are not alone. This sort of presence is often reported at Rikard's Mill, and visitors will tend to experience the unsettling feeling of being watched even when there are no others in the area. Physical manifestations of whatever haunts Rikard's Mill are rare. But is there anything more disturbing than being in a room all by yourself and yet knowing that you're not alone?

Old Courthouse Museum

You've probably never been there, but there's a good chance you would recognize the courtroom in the old Monroe County Courthouse. Built in 1903, it played a pivotal role in a little book by an author who never published anything else: *To Kill a Mockingbird*. Not only was the scene in that book based on the courtroom itself, but when the movie was made from the book, the set designer also came to Monroeville to measure, photograph and draw the courtroom before re-creating it on a Hollywood sound stage. And

Front view of the Old Courthouse Museum. *Courtesy Lee Peacock.*

no wonder: when she was a child, Harper Lee would often entertain herself by watching her father practice law in this very courtroom.

Several years ago, the museum would do haunted tours of Monroeville around Halloween, including the courthouse. Guides, dressed fully in old-style clothes, would share stories of hauntings. Famous though it may be, it is only those who have spent lonely nights in the courthouse's upper chambers that know how truly unsettling it can be there. Whispers waft in the breeze, even when there is no one to make them and no breeze to carry them. The sounds are those of another era, and the pungent smell of pipe tobacco smoke is thick and unyielding, even though smoking is strictly prohibited in the building today.

The former director of the museum would often find herself working late at night. More than once, she'd get the feeling that she wasn't alone, or she would hear sounds in the distance that seemed to portend an intruder. And yet, every time she went to find whoever was making the noises, she would come up empty-handed.

Whence do these manifestations come, and what drives them? Sometimes, even the most famous places keep their secrets close.

McConnico Cemetery

You do not hear them before you see them. There is no thundering of their horse's hooves, no echoing in your ears, no warning that you are about to be trampled into the dust. But then you see them: two columns of Union soldiers, riding at full gallop, searching always for the man who laid them low and mutilated their bodies. And to make matters all the worse? It is through one of Monroe County's oldest cemeteries that they ride.

It was 1865, and tensions were running high throughout the South. Appomattox had fallen, and Lee had surrendered. Stories ran wild that Jefferson Davis was on the lam, trying to make it to South America. Defeat hung in the air, and the lands still controlled by the Confederate army were rapidly shrinking. The same story was being told in Alabama.

After Mobile fell and the Union army began sweeping up through southern Alabama, town after town fell, many burned to the ground. But even though the Union army moved from victory to victory, there was something they feared—the name of a single man: Lafayette Seigler.

Seigler, a native of Claiborne, had watched with horror as his beloved Alabama was invaded, plundered and razed by Union soldiers. And eventually, he simply had enough. He decided to launch his own war on the Northern forces. And like a character from a Hollywood movie, he did just that.

What could Seigler do against the combined might of the Union that armies of Rebels had failed to do? He had two advantages. First, he was alone and could disappear into the countryside he knew so well before anyone even realized he had been in the area. And two, he owned the fastest horse in Monroe County—some say the fastest horse in the whole state. And that fact dictated his strategy.

First, Seigler would find Union cavalrymen, preferably a lone rider on his own. Then he'd get his attention. Maybe he cursed at him. Maybe he fired a shot over his head. Invariably, the soldier, his honor challenged, would give chase. Seigler would use his speed to gain the upper ground, and then he'd wait on the hapless Union soldier to stumble into his trap.

That he killed men was a given, but Seigler knew that murdering a soldier here or there would have no impact on the war. He also knew that terror was his greatest weapon. And so, he decided to inflict it with maximum cruelty. Sometimes he would smear the dead man's blood on his saddle and send the riderless horse back to camp. But his favorite tactic was to leave the body somewhere that he knew it would be found—with one critical item missing. Before he abandoned the man's body, he'd first take his ears, severing them from the dead soldier's head. Throughout history, desperadoes have kept track of the men they killed through one method or another. Seigler wore the ears of his victims cured and tied on a leather thong around his neck.

Union officials were determined to find the man and stop him. They placed a bounty on his head, a princely sum if reports from the time were to be believed, and they promised any man who found Seigler that the reward would be his, whether they brought the bandit in dead or alive. But old Lafayette Seigler was simply too good and his horse too fast. Despite some close calls, he was never found, and the bodies of Union soldiers continued to pile up until the very last day of the war.

How many did he kill? It's impossible to say anymore. All we know for certain is that a company of cavalrymen—twelve strong—was buried in the old graveyard deep in the woods of Monroe County, just outside Claiborne, called McConnico Cemetery. And it is there, among the centuries-old tombstones, that visitors see to this day the columns of gray riders, mounted still on their horses, searching for something or someone.

They ride in the darkest hours of the night, before the first rays of the new dawn break across the cemetery. All are astride beautiful gray horses. All are dressed in fine blue uniforms with polished buttons that shine like burnished bronze. All twelve wear white gloves, their hands resting on the pommels of their saddles, the reins of their horses hanging loose. They ride in utter and eerie silence. There are no hoof beats, no sound of horses neighing, no clanking of their swords against the harness of their saddles. If they come upon an obstacle, they divide into columns of six and ride around it before coming back together and continuing on their way. And perhaps most unusual of all, each wears a bandage around his head, wrapped securely about the ears and tied beneath the chin.

They were seen first in the autumn of 1865, after the War Between the States had come to an end. This first sighting is well documented. It is said that a couple from the city of Claiborne, Charles and Barbara Locklin, were traveling to southern Alabama in the early morning hours, before the sun had even risen, when they came to the borders of McConnico Cemetery. It was then that they saw the two columns of soldiers, the couple's normally quiet and calm steeds going wild as the bafflingly silent cavalry passed. And then the men simply vanished into thin air.

Their story has been repeated down through the centuries. The details never change. The riders always number twelve and always ride in determined silence, as if they are searching.

No one knows what became of old Lafayette Seigler after the war. Some say that he simply dissolved back into society, becoming a moderately successful farmer and living to his old age. Others say that he moved out west to settle a new territory, that his home of Alabama was never the same after the horrors of war—many of which he was responsible for perpetrating.

But there are others who claim that Seigler's disappearance can be attributed to another, more esoteric cause. And if they are to be believed, the riders found their quarry, and by the time they had finished with him, they had taken far more than his ears. But if that is true, why do the riders still haunt the early hours of Monroe County? Perhaps they still search for the missing pieces of their bodies; perhaps they can only rest in peace if they can find the ears that were taken from them a century and a half ago.

Until then, they ride on, silently, through the darkened night, ever longing, ever searching.

Claiborne Masonic Lodge

In a county filled with historical structures, perhaps none is more notable than the Masonic Lodge in the ghost town of Claiborne. The oldest building in all of Monroe County, the lodge was erected at Claiborne on a spot overlooking the Alabama River. Funds for its construction were raised by public lottery, and the upper floor was dedicated to the use of the Lodge. The lower floor, however, had any number of uses, including the city's town hall, a school, a church and even a courtroom. It was in this courtroom that William B. Travis—a Mason in his own right—practiced law.

The name of William Travis is probably less familiar than what he did. He failed as a teacher. He failed as a lawyer. He failed as a parent and husband. But as a hero, he has few equals.

On March 5, 1836, Colonel William Barret Travis stood in the courtyard of an old Spanish mission in San Antonio, Texas, and drew a line in the sand. Twenty-four hours later, he and all the men who crossed that line would be dead, but the legend of the Alamo would live on forever.

And it wasn't just William Travis who graced the halls of the Claiborne Masonic Lodge. In March 1825, one of America's greatest heroes of the Revolutionary War visited Alabama and Monroe County. And interestingly enough, he wasn't even an American.

He was born Marie-Joseph Paul Yves Roch Gilbert du Motier, but as if that wasn't enough of a name, he was known to the world as the Marquis de Lafayette. He was raised in wealth and privilege, the son of a hero after his father was killed in battle. He boarded at the finest French schools in Paris before moving on to the military academy. By the time he was fourteen, Lafayette followed his father into the service of the king, commissioned as a second lieutenant in the Royal Guard—the Musketeers. Within a few years, he had been promoted to captain and transferred to the Noailles Dragoons Regiment. It was there that he became acquainted with the Masonic Order, and ideas of freedom and the rights of man began to take hold. The Declaration of Independence was just the sort of thing that would inspire such a young man.

The Americans offered him the rank of major general, but his father-in-law was not interested in seeing his daughter's husband run off on some foolish quest for liberty. So he had Lafayette assigned to the worst possible place for an American patriot: Great Britain. But Lafayette was determined. Without his father-in-law's knowledge, he returned to France and managed to purchase a ship to take him to America. But there were some eyes that he could not escape, and King Louis XVI, learning of the young Marquis' intentions, forbade him to follow through on his plans. Lafayette, however, could not be deterred. He launched an audacious escape from France, evading both army and naval efforts to stop him. On June 13, 1777, he landed in South Carolina and made his way to Philadelphia.

Initially, he had problems getting on with a unit. By this point, the colonies had been overrun by young Frenchmen looking to make their name in the world so that they might impress the ladies back home. But Lafayette managed to charm the most important person in Philadelphia: Benjamin Franklin. On behalf of the young Frenchman, Franklin sent a letter to George Washington, and before long, Lafayette had become the general's aide-de-camp.

Lafayette would come to be an invaluable asset. Not only did he prove himself again and again in battle, but when the French eventually did join the cause, he was also an irreplaceable negotiator for the American cause—at least once the king forgave him for his earlier disobedience. So important to the American war effort was Lafayette that the British put a price on his head and sent five thousand men to track him down when they learned that he was near Philadelphia. When Yorktown fell to the Americans, Lafayette was there. When the British surrendered, Lafayette was there. So great was the mark that Lafayette left on the consciousness of the new country that when the Americans came to the aide of France in World War I, the aide to General John Pershing is said to have remarked, "Nous voila, Lafayette!" (Lafayette, we are here!)

Lafayette's life continued to be one of intrigue and interest. He went from being one of the king's closest advisors to a leader in the Revolution to almost its victim. When the Second French Revolution overthrew the government in 1830, Lafayette was offered the dictatorship of France. He turned it down, dying in 1834.

During his life, though, he never forgot his love for America. In 1824, he returned to take a grand tour of the fledgling nation, accompanied by his son, George Washington Lafayette. And one of his stops was the Masonic Lodge in Claiborne.

The old Lodge in Claiborne is a reminder of an older time. The village is deserted now, a ghost town, the victim of changing times. Perhaps with all of this history, it's no surprise that the Masonic Lodge is reputed to be haunted. The exact details of that haunting are never clear. Some say that there are noises at night within the empty building. Others claim that there are lights (orbs) that float through the air around it. Some claim that there is no ghost at all—just the eerie visage of a once prominent place now left to fade away into nothing.

Monroe County Public Library

On Pineville Road in Monroeville sits the Monroe County Public Library, established in 1984. But its history is much older than that. Before it was a library, the building was a hotel—the LaSalle Hotel. Its most famous guest is perhaps Gregory Peck, who visited Monroeville in the '60s while getting ready for his role in *To Kill a Mockingbird*. And more than a few visitors to the property have described strange and unusual events.

You wouldn't know it when you enter the sunlit ground floor of the library. But once you leave the light behind and ascend to the darkened second floor, any feeling of warmth quickly disappears, replaced by an overwhelming sense of foreboding. The full range of paranormal occurrences has been recorded here, from unexplained lights to disembodied voices and footsteps with no possible owner.

Surely, hundreds of guests passed through the old hotel's doors. If there are records of murders or deaths within its walls, they have long since been lost. But if the stories of those who have spent lonely afternoons in the upper corridors of the library are to be believed, many of the guests who checked in never bothered to check out.

L&N Railroad Tunnel

In the middle of a forest deep in the wilds of Monroe County, there's an old train tunnel. Built in 1899, the tunnel is almost nine hundred feet long. It was constructed by four crews of fifteen men each that worked day and night to complete the tunnel. Train service has long since ended along the tracks that still run through the dark woods of the county, but the tunnel remains. It is an open maw, a dark and foreboding place that seems to scream, "Stay out!"

Perhaps there is a reason. The tunnel was critical to the running of the L&N Railroad at the time of its construction. It was for this reason that so much work was put into building it quickly. It is said that one crew started the work from the north side, while the others approached from the south. The men worked with simple tools, and they did not take many precautions for the safety of those who worked with thousands of tons of earth just above their heads. It is perhaps a miracle that the whole mountain didn't come down on top of them. But small cave-ins were common and sometimes fatal. The records from that era are not very good, and we don't know how many men went to their deaths in the darkness of that endless night. But it cannot be doubted that some did die.

There are several ghosts said to haunt the tunnel. The first is called the "headless conductor." Legend says that the conductor was having an affair with one of the engineers' wives. The engineer found out, and one day, when the conductor stuck his head out of the train to check some valves, the engineer fired the engine, lurching the train into the L&N tunnel. The conductor was too slow to respond, and off came his head.

Another story revolves around a train called the Famous 14, the train that inspired Hank Williams's song "The Old Log Train." The story goes that a woman from Chapman was on the train, headed to meet her husband, who was on the way home from the First World War. As the train was nearing the tunnel, she realized that her child was missing. Just as she was passing from one carriage to another, the train disappeared into the tunnel. The woman lost her footing and fell to her death, crushed beneath

Front view of the L&N Railroad tunnel. *Courtesy Lee Peacock.*

the wheels of the train. It is said that visitors to the tunnel at night can hear the screams of the woman from the tunnel and the sound of her crying as she searches for her baby, and you will even see a glowing figure walking up and down the tracks.

If you go down to the old L&N Tunnel today, most likely all that you will find is thousands and thousands of small bats that now make the tunnel their home. But if you are lucky—or perhaps unlucky—you will hear the ghostly cries of those who died within the tunnel. And if you go inside to see where the voice comes from, well, who knows what you might find.

MONTGOMERY COUNTY

Montgomery, Alabama. Cradle of the Confederacy. Heated battleground of the civil rights era. And the place a writer nobody had ever heard of named Francis Scott Key Fitzgerald met a girl named Zelda.

Montgomery, in addition to being the capital of the state of Alabama, is as deep as the Black Warrior River in history and legend. Interestingly, Montgomery County and the city of Montgomery are named after two different people. Montgomery County gets its moniker from Lemuel P. Montgomery, a soldier killed at the Battle of Horseshoe Bend. It was at that battle that Andrew Jackson decisively defeated the British-allied Creek Indians, ending their resistance and effectively opening Alabama for colonization. The city of Montgomery, on the other hand, is named for Richard Montgomery, a Revolutionary War general killed during the failed attempt to capture Quebec City, Canada, from the British. Two wars against England, two different men named Montgomery killed. Born in devotion to country and defending the United States, Montgomery would soon be at the center of the effort to tear the Union apart.

It is hard to imagine today what it must have been like in those dark days in April 1865. Four years earlier, things had been very different across the South. For decades, the fissures between the Southern states and their Northern brethren had grown increasingly unsalvageable with every passing year. Rooted in the question of slavery, Northern and Southern politicians formed political blocs based more on regional loyalty than the type of issue-based disagreements we experience today. In Congress, power was divided between slave states and free states, with the Southern bloc garnering extra representation in the House of Representatives due to its slave population. The uneasy truce between the blocs could only have lasted as long as the equilibrium was maintained. But the United States was a country on the move, and westward expansion would almost destroy it.

With the victory of the United States over Mexico in 1848 and the Gadsden Purchase of 1853, the nation gained huge swaths of territory for settlement. The settlers came, driven by the belief in Manifest Destiny that was widespread at the time. Soon, states were ready to be admitted to the Union, and the question had to be answered—would they be free or slave?

The addition of a free state without a slave state to counterbalance it would lead to a shift in power in Congress. The Civil War didn't start until the election of Abraham Lincoln, but the breakup began much earlier. Decades before and leading up to secession, the territories were engaged in bloody internecine warfare, struggles to determine which side—slave or free—the state would join upon its entry into the nation. Men such as John Brown led paramilitary actions that led to monikers like "Bleeding Kansas." With bands of marauders killing one another and John Brown's execution after an assault on Harper's Ferry that he intended to use to spur a slave revolt, things had reached a breaking point. Many people in states both north and south of the Mason-Dixon line were simply looking for an excuse to separate. The election of Abraham Lincoln in 1860 gave them that excuse. Alabama helped lead the way.

Politics in 1860 were dominated in Alabama by the so-called Fire Eaters, led by William Lowndes Yancey. Yancey helped split the Democratic Party in two, leading a walkout of the Alabama contingent of the party's convention in Charleston. Many of the other Southern delegations went with him, and a divided Democratic Party could never contend with the newly minted Republicans and their Free Soil platform. But Abraham Lincoln did not carry a single slaveholding state. In fact, in the fifteen states that allowed slavery, Lincoln won just 2 counties out of 996, both in Missouri. In Alabama, no ballots were cast for Lincoln.

South Carolina was the first state to issue an article of secession. Alabama followed close behind. The state of Alabama and its people were committed to the cause of Southern independence, and when the votes were tallied in Montgomery, the decision to abandon the Union was decided once and for all. In February 1861, delegates from the secessionist states met in Montgomery to formally establish their new government, with the city as the first capital. The die was cast, and the South would burn for it.

At first, the South won battle after battle as superior leadership overcame deficits in manpower and war matériel. Names like Manassas and Chancellorsville gave the Southern partisans hope that perhaps they could defeat the North after all. In time, however, a combination of the vast advantages held by the Union as well as the emergence of generals like William Tecumseh Sherman and Ulysses S. Grant turned the tide for the North. Four years later, the initial jubilation that Southerners felt had turned to bitter sorrow and devastation.

In August 1864, Union admiral David G. Farragut gave the now famous command, "Damn the torpedoes, full speed ahead!" during what would come to be known as the Battle of Mobile Bay. His words had barely faded before the Union army was on the march north. By April 1865, the war was all but over. More than 1 million men had been killed or wounded, and much of the South was aflame, burning to the ground. Even the University of Alabama in the north, the educational pride and joy of the state, was destroyed.

The period of Reconstruction followed, with anti-Union paramilitary groups springing up to fight perceived abuses by federal soldiers and to generally torture the black population of freed slaves. Soon the Ku Klux Klan was born. For more than one hundred years, white hooded riders turned the nights into fiery flights of terror. Crosses—and often people—were burned, and a new status quo was established in which segregation, both de facto and by law, was put in place of the old slave system.

It was in Montgomery that the power of the Klan was felt most visibly, but it was also in Montgomery that this power was finally broken. It started with the efforts of people both famous and unknown, of Martin Luther King and Rosa Parks, of Freedom Riders and sit-in protestors. By the year 2000, the various Klan organizations were bankrupt, bled dry by lawsuits for their violent attacks, most brought by the Southern Poverty Law Center of Morris Dees, headquartered in Montgomery.

With all that history, it is no surprise that Montgomery has many locations where unexplained happenings are all too commonplace. In fact, Montgomery County is so haunted that one could fill a whole book with them, which is exactly what Faith Serafin has done in her collection *Haunted Montgomery*. Check it out, if you dare.

The Red Lady of Huntingdon College

She walks the halls of Pratt Hall at Huntingdon College, an eerie red glow floating in her wake. She is an apparition of terror, a frightening phantom that turns the blood cold of all who see her. She is the Red Lady. And interestingly enough, there's more than one.

The first Red Lady was reported when Huntingdon College was still Tuskegee Female College. It was a particularly dark night in the late 1800s. The girls of the dorm known as Sky Alley were still awake, even if "lights out" had been called quite a bit earlier in the evening. It was then that they noticed a glowing red light that seemed to float down the hall, pouring in through cracks under their doors. Some of the more intrepid young women opened their doors and peeked out into the hallway. They witnessed an apparition unlike anything they had ever before seen—a banshee, a ghostly woman in an elegant crimson gown, carrying a matching parasol as she glided down the corridor as if it were her debutante ball. She did not look to the left or the right, nor did she seem to notice those about her. It was as if she were in her own world. According to the girls, she passed up and down the hall until the sun broke over the eastern horizon, at which point she vanished.

Why did the woman appear? Where did she go? The students never knew, and the Lady in Red never returned—at least not *that* Lady in Red.

In 1910, the campus moved to the Montgomery location where it now resides, renamed the Woman's College of Alabama. The Red Lady was forgotten, and perhaps her legend would have faded forever into obscurity were it not for a young girl named Margaret who would give the legend of the Red Lady a terrifying twist.

Margaret—or, depending on whom you believe, Martha—was the daughter of two transplanted Southerners. Both her parents were natives of Alabama, but the family had moved to New York to pursue lucrative business opportunities. When it came time for Margaret to go to college, there was only one school that would do: Huntingdon, the Woman's College of Alabama, where Margaret's mother had attended in her girlhood. Margaret was not a happy young lady. She did not want to leave New York City, particularly for the backwaters of her parents' home state. But in the end, what choice did she have? She agreed to follow her father and mother's wishes, and down to Alabama she went.

The thing that struck Margaret's classmates when she arrived on campus was not her aloof attitude or her Yankee ways, although both would soon

Pratt Hall's "Red Lady." *Courtesy Brandon Stoker.*

make an impression. No, it was the color red. She had a deep fondness for crimson. Her clothes were red. Her bedspread, rug and decorations were all bathed in a dark-red hue. It was rare that she was seen in or out of Pratt Hall and not clothed in crimson garments.

Needless to say, Margaret was not exactly popular on campus. She was a northerner, and a wealthy one to boot. It didn't help that she was also painfully shy and not given to seeking out new friends. Loneliness became her watchword, and depression followed quickly. Soon she was very unhappy, with nary a friend to lift the burden of her sadness. And that made her a very unpopular roommate.

Weeks turned into months, and still, no one wanted to live with Margaret. Finally, the girl who had been elected the president of Pratt Hall agreed that she would take up residence with the lonely, unpopular student. By all reports, Margaret's new roommate did everything she could to become friends with the poor girl, but it was not to be. Eventually, even she became beaten down by the atmosphere of sadness and depression that clung about Margaret, and she decided to move out. It is said that when she did that, Margaret gave her a solemn warning: she would regret leaving Margaret behind, and neither she nor Huntingdon would ever forget it.

Margaret withdrew even more into herself. She stayed in her room, only venturing out late at night, well after "lights out," her red cloak wrapped tight around her. She would stop at random rooms, opening the unlocked doors and staring into the rooms of her hall mates. Needless to say, it was a bizarre and unsettling experience for all involved.

And then came the day when Margaret didn't show up for classes. She didn't come to any meals. Some of the girls met, and it was decided that her old roommate—the dorm president—should go check on her. The girl made her way up the steps of the dorm stairway, every footfall harder and harder to make, each step seemingly bringing her closer to some unknown doom. When she reached the hallway, she could see an eerie red glow emanating from Margaret's room. Then she opened the door.

Margaret was inside. She was wrapped in a red robe, and she had pulled the red bedspread around her. But it was the greater pool of red that made the poor girl who found her grow sick—the pool of blood that spread out around the dead girl's body. She had slashed her wrists.

They buried Margaret, but her spirit never left the fourth floor of Pratt Hall. Every year, a new group of girls enrolls at Huntingdon College. And every year, more and more of them see the ghost of the Red Lady, walking up and down the hallway where she died. They say that a red light still emanates from beneath the door of her old room, disappearing as soon as you open it. Why does she haunt the place where she died? Why does she stay at the location of the worst days of her life? No one can be sure. All we know is that the Red Lady of Huntingdon College is waiting, and as long as there are new students to meet, she will never be alone.

Perry County

The tiny county of Perry was named after Commodore Oliver Hazard Perry, the hero of Lake Erie. Perry was in command of the Great Lake fleet that took on the British during the War of 1812. Staying true to the motto of his flagship, "Don't give up the ship," Perry's naval brilliance resulted in the utter defeat of his Royal Navy adversaries, leading to his famous missive to General William Henry Harrison: "We have met the enemy and they are ours." It was the first time in history that an entire British naval squadron had surrendered. Perry's victory was one of the key turning points of the war, helping to lead to the eventual American victory.

The darkest moment in Perry County's history helped lead to one of the major events of the civil rights movement. In 1965, Jimmie Lee Jackson, an unarmed African American man, was shot dead by a white state trooper. His death inspired the Selma–Montgomery march for equality.

Marion Military Institute

Of all the military junior colleges in the country, none is older than Marion Military Institute. Throughout the Civil War, world wars and into the modern day, Marion has continued on, training young men to become soldiers.

Marion was initially attached to Howard College, but it became its own independent institute when Howard moved to Birmingham and was rechristened Samford. Some faculty stayed behind, and they formed the basis for Marion Military. But like so many places we visit throughout the Black Belt, it was the Civil War that made Marion Military a place of ghostly legend.

It was toward the end of the war, and the Confederate forces were vastly outnumbered. In battle after battle, they were overwhelmed and outgunned. Many of these battles were routs, even massacres. The armies needed somewhere to send their wounded and dying. Marion became one of those places. As the casualties mounted, battle victims were taken to the chapel on campus, which was turned into a hospice—a place where men went to die. They turned the open field behind the church into a graveyard. And that is why the Marion Military Institute remains haunted to this day.

How many died on the campus? How many are buried there? It is impossible to say. But what is absolutely clear is that campus cadets are all too familiar with the spirits that haunt their campus and walk the halls of their dorms. Many have seen objects in their room move as if on their own. Footsteps, whispers, laughs and cries echo down the hallways. No one ever feels alone in Marion. In fact, some cadets even find themselves driven slightly mad by the spirits that haunt the school, with formerly solid students experiencing violent mood swings and deep depression.

Yes, Marion has much history to boast of. But sometimes, history has unwanted side effects.

Moore-Webb-Holmes Plantation

Just outside Marion sits the enigmatic Moore-Webb-Holmes Plantation, one of the last active plantations in the state—it appears as though it has simply always been there. Owned by the same family since William "the wagon maker" Moore moved to Alabama from South Carolina in 1819, just as the territory became a state, the farm grew from the original eighty acres that Moore homesteaded into thousands upon thousands of acres of fertile soil.

William Moore was productive in more ways than one. He and his wife were the parents of eleven children. Down through the decades, the farm has remained in the family's hands, passing from one generation to the next down to the present day. The family still has the original deed to the property, signed by Andrew Jackson himself.

The original homesite—the family home tragically burned down in 1927—houses a veritable museum of historical artifacts and buildings. These relics of the past include the log seed house used with the first cotton gin, a carriage house, a smokehouse, a chicken coop, a potato house with a pit for the storage of vegetables and many more of the necessary buildings of a nineteenth-century plantation, including an overseer's house and slave quarters. It's no surprise that many of these buildings have stories, oftentimes paranormal ones.

One of those stories starts on Christmas Day. The family had decided to host a Christmas party, and it must have been attended by at least one hundred people. Once it ended, the family was talking about how much they enjoyed the event when their eyes were drawn to the hallway. There was a woman in a long white gown, not the type normally associated with this day and age. She was walking down the hall—or rather, *floating*.

It wasn't the first time the people of the plantation had felt the presence of the long since dead. In fact, one might say that the family never feels alone. Doors open on their own. Reflections in mirrors appear and then vanish before your eyes. But it is this woman in white who is most often reported, drifting along from room to room, vanishing before witnesses' eyes. Every generation of the Moore family has seen her. Perhaps she has something to do with the large bloodstain at the foot of the grand staircase. Even in a place where the history is well known, the centuries create mysteries.

Westwood Plantation

Westwood Plantation has a long and illustrious history, marked by one of the most prominent families in the early United States. In 1839, twenty-five-year-old James Lewis Price made his way from Virginia down to Uniontown, Alabama. He came to Perry County with his fortune already intact but with every intention of growing it all the more. Price had the pedigree to make it happen.

The son of John Fleming Price and Maria Overton Winston Price (keeping a lady's more prestigious name after marriage is not entirely a modern invention), Price would have grown up regaled with tales of how his family was one of the most prominent of the Old Dominion state in the days of the Revolution. When his father died when Price was only three years old, the family became even more well-to-do. Price's mother did not a widow remain. Instead, she married William Marshall, the younger brother of U.S. Supreme Court chief justice John Marshall and a man of some repute in his own right. It goes without saying that Price did not go hungry as a child.

When he came of age, he attended the University of Virginia and there obtained a law degree—a nearly superfluous addition to his repertoire given the future direction of his life. Perry apparently felt stifled in Richmond, where everything was presented to him on a silver platter, and with that in mind, he departed for the "Wild Wild West" of Alabama to establish himself and be his own man.

Of course, it helped that he had his father's inheritance to help ease his entry into Alabama society. Once he arrived in Uniontown, he purchased a plot of Black Belt land and decided to build a plantation called Westwood—named for a similar home in Virginia that had belonged to his grandfather. He built the home out of the pine timbers that his slaves cleared off the property to make way for the cotton crop that would be grown there. Price had an eye for property; Westwood sits on the highest point between the Alabama River in Selma and the Black Warrior River in Demopolis. Westwood would preside like a castle over the land, and Price would be king of all he surveyed.

Price hired a French architect to design his new home (because why not?), one who took advantage of both the Greek Revival style popular in the area as well as the more subtle Italianate school. Price's army of slaves was once again put to work, this time to build the house that would be his home. Within four years, it was finished, and there were few that would doubt the slaves' skill, precision or dedication to their task.

Price truly spared no expense, and to visit Westwood today is to walk into the heart of true southern elegance. The house is home to no fewer than six bedrooms, eight covered porches and a number of flat-roofed decks accessible from the second floor that would have allowed Price's guests not only to enjoy the beautiful weather of a southern spring or fall but also to gaze out across the vast expanse that the house commands.

Of course, Price could only have the luxuries that money could buy at the time. There was no electricity in those days, no indoor plumbing and no central heating or air conditioning. So, Price made do as best he could. Westwood has three brick chimneys to service the ten fireplaces that would have kept the denizens of the house warm during the not too terrible southern Alabama winters. The summers were obviously more of a challenge. Price met it with floor-to-ceiling windows that could be lowered from above and raised from the bottom to provide a cool breeze. Rainwater was diverted into large cisterns for general household use, while a well provided drinking water and a deep underground chamber provided the refrigeration necessary to keep food from spoiling.

Price was nothing but a success during his days in Alabama. He had a plan to bring the railroad to the Black Belt, a goal that he accomplished as the founder and president of the Alabama and Mississippi Rivers Railroad Company. The railroad brought money and commerce, but it also brought political power to Uniontown. To this day, Westwood remains in the care of Price's descendants. It was a successful life indeed.

Is it possible that Price accomplished so much in life that he never wanted to leave it behind?

They say that the nights at Westwood are never quiet. It's hard to separate truth from fiction, given that Westwood remains privately owned by the Price family. But rumors spread quickly through small southern towns. They say that the ghost of Price still paces the halls, as if he is waiting on a business transaction to complete that hasn't quite come through. Strange spirit lights have been witnessed, hovering around the many open expanses of the roof, as if someone is still staring out over an empire that once belonged to the master of Westwood mansion.

But you know how it is. Stories are just stories. Sometimes.

Judson College

In 1838, the good members of Siloam Baptist Church decided that Alabama needed a place for the higher education of women. The University of Alabama, while ahead of its time, still wouldn't admit its first coed until 1892, after all. It was through this effort that the Judson Female Institute was born. The college's namesake, Ann Hasseltine Judson, was a true pioneer, credited with being America's first female foreign missionary. In only a few years, the founders of the college had commissioned and constructed a massive four-story building to serve as the heart of the campus, named Jewett Hall after the school's first president, Dr. Milo P. Jewett.

For several decades, the college operated without incident. Even the fires of the Civil War did not serve to destroy what the teachers and students of Judson had created. The same, unfortunately, could not be said for the fires inside the chimneys of Jewett Hall. In 1888, one of those fires did what several thousand Yankees had not: burn the college to the ground. The women of Judson were not deterred. Within months, the new Jewett Hall was rising.

The women of Judson acquitted themselves well during the world wars, serving as nurses and Red Cross workers on the battlefields. Then, in 1947, fire struck again, this time when lightning hit the dome of Jewett Hall. And once again, the building was totally destroyed. And so, in its place, Jewett the third was to rise, a building that remains to this day, no doubt despite the efforts of fire and flame.

One thing that the fires of Jewett have not managed to burn away are the stories of supernatural activity at Judson. Young women who are assigned room 313 in Judson are said to move in with more than a small feeling of unease. Everyone at Judson knows that 313 is haunted. On a hot summer night when the rest of the campus is sweltering, room 313 is bathed in frigid air. More than one lone roommate has claimed to have heard whispers in the otherwise empty room. Items move, rearrange themselves or disappear altogether. What is the cause of these hauntings?

One particularly grisly tale centers on a young girl who lived in 313 who decided to sneak in her boyfriend for a late-night "study session." When the dorm mother heard, she was furious. She went looking for the girl and her beau. The boy fled before she arrived, and desperate to escape, he tried the elevator. Unfortunately for him, it was stuck between floors. The boy pried open the doors and hid on top of the elevator. After the young lady managed to convince her dorm mother that nothing was amiss, she went to find her young man. And when she did, she pressed the elevator button. Up the elevator came, crushing her screaming boyfriend and killing him instantly. We've heard worse reasons to stick around a place, though.

Of course, many claim that the stories of haunted 313 are nothing more than the overactive imagination of teenage girls. How, then, to explain the ghost of Kirtley Hall, believed by students, alumni, faculty and staff alike? Well, that one is more complicated.

Kirtley Hall is named after Anne Kirtley, one of Judson College's most beloved professors. Kirtley was responsible for many of the campus's traditions and was said to be a devoted lady. And like clockwork, the door to Kirtley Hall is said to open and close before chapel service, opening again when chapel service comes to a conclusion. The ghost of Kirtley—readily recognizable because of the portrait of her that hangs on the college grounds and occasionally moves without human interaction—has been seen all over campus by dozens of students and teachers, everywhere from rooms in Kirtley Hall to classrooms to elevators.

Is it any surprise that a place with as much history as Judson College can't seem to outrun it?

Carlisle Hall

So many of our stories are about houses, places that seem to teem with unnatural energy. That energy too often goes without a name of its own, just another of God's creatures that has danced its short piece on this world's stage, only to pass into oblivion. But not Carlisle Hall. There we know the ghost that stays behind, tormented by the events of long ago. Her name is Anna.

Anna Carlisle grew up in the home that bears her family's name with the carefree spirit that all of us hope our children can enjoy. She wanted for nothing, and every day she would go to play in the mighty tower that overlooked the whole property. But she did not play alone. A neighbor boy would go with her. What started out as a childhood friendship would grow into a love—young, pure and strong. "One day," she would tell him, "when we are grown up, we'll marry. And then our children will play in the tower just like we always did."

And maybe that's what would have happened had life not intervened in their love. For it was late 1860, and the winds of war were blowing through Alabama. When it came, the man who loved Anna with all his heart had to put her aside for duty, honor and love of his country. And she, loving him as she did, never blamed him for that decision.

He met her at her home one final time, dressed in the gray of a Confederate officer. He promised that he would marry her when he returned. But she asked one other thing of him, one other promise. She asked for a sign. His slave, a young man whom both of them had grown up with and loved as a brother, would wait to hear the outcome of the battles in which her lover would fight. If he survived, then the slave would ride to the plantation waving a white flag. But if he died, then he would carry a red flag. Anna promised to wait in the tower for the news, and despite his protestations, her husband-to-be could do nothing but grant her this one wish.

Off he went, and as she watched him ride away on his horse from the top of the great tower, she prayed to God that he would return. She continued that prayer for days and weeks on end. Her family would visit her in the tower, bring her food and beg her to come down to the house below. But from the moment the sun burst above the horizon to the last instant before it dipped below the trees, Anna waited.

How many other young women across Alabama, Tennessee, Ohio, Massachusetts, Virginia and Mississippi waited with her? How many young boys died on the battlefield with the name of their beloved on their lips? How many hearts were broken in such a way that they could never love again?

The day came, as of course it must have. Anna heard the sound of a galloping horse. She steeled herself for what she might see, but nothing could tear her eyes away from the bend in the road where the rider was rapidly approaching. And then he was there—bearing a dark-red flag above his head, the crimson color of blood.

We can't say for how long Anna stared at that harbinger of doom, how long she stood mesmerized by the one thing she had prayed with all her heart she would never see. All we know for sure is that Anna cried out, the sound of a young girl's heart breaking, before she threw herself from the top of the tower, falling down, down, down to her death.

The tower is still there at Carlisle, and so is Anna. On quiet nights, when the sun hangs low in the western sky, you just might hear the unmistakable sound of hoof beats pounding through the coming dusk. And then, as thunder must follow the lightning, the soul-rending, heartbreaking cry of a woman who lived only to die.

Part III
Western Black Belt

Choctaw County

Some of the counties in Alabama have attempted to forget their Native American heritage. Others, like Choctaw County, embrace it. The Choctaw Indian tribe—after which the county was named—were part of the Mississippian culture, builders of great earthen mounds that hardly fail to impress even today. The Choctaws were known as one of the "Five Civilized Tribes" because of their willingness to adapt to the European culture that was coming to dominate the Americas. During the Revolutionary War, the Choctaws were one of the few tribes to side with the colonies against the English. In the end, neither adaptation nor loyalty in time of war did them much good; they were the first tribe to lose their land under Andrew Jackson's infamous Indian Removal Act of 1830.

While Presidents George Washington and Thomas Jefferson had encouraged cohabitation with friendly native tribes, Jackson was more interested in having the land for settlement and exploitation. Many tribes would suffer as a result. The Choctaws just so happened to be the first. After the Treaty of Dancing Rabbit Creek stripped them of their lands, a Choctaw chief by the name of Thomas Harkins was quoted as saying that the action would lead to a "trail of tears and death," a phrase that was as prophetic then as it is iconic now.

Bladon Springs Cemetery

At Bladon Springs Cemetery, on the shore of the mighty Tombigbee, there is a grave that belongs to one Norman A. Staples. His life—and his death—was one of great promise and sudden failure. Norman's father, James, had a dream. He would build the grandest steamboat the rivers of Alabama had ever seen. And that he did. James designed the boat himself, taking care to make sure that every aspect was as elegant as it could be. By all measures, he succeeded, and in 1908, his ship was launched to great fanfare.

Sadly, James didn't get to captain his ship. Soon he was dead, and ownership of the proud vessel passed to his son, Norman. He had not commanded the boat known as the *James T. Staples* for long before he found himself sailing in a river of red ink. What led to his financial difficulties? Some say it was the efforts of his competitors, who, so committed to dominating the trade on the river, were even willing to sabotage Norman. But more likely it was simply changing times. The age of the great steamships had passed even before James had put his boat on the water. In reality, this failure was probably inevitable.

But whatever the case may be, in December 1912, Norman's creditors acted, seizing his beloved *James T. Staples* and selling it at auction, some say to the very company that had plotted Norman's downfall. It was too much for Norman to bear. On January 2, 1913, Norman put a shotgun against his chest and pulled the trigger. He was buried at Bladon Springs Cemetery.

Not three days after his body was laid in the dirt, crew members on the *James T. Staples* began to see things they could not explain. Some claimed that the disembodied spirit of their dead captain walked the ship at night. The entire crew quit in fear. New men were hired. They, too, reported the spirit, but perhaps because they did not know him, they stayed on the job.

But then something happened that was truly horrifying for a man who makes his trade on the river. The next time the boat docked, every rat on the ship came like a flood off the decks, down to the shoreline, and fled. On January 12, the last reported appearance of the spirit of Norman Staple was said to have occurred in the boiler room, below decks. The stage was set for tragedy.

On January 13, 1913, the ship docked at Powe's Landing to take on fuel and supplies. At the very hour that Captain Staples killed himself, the boiler—the one his spirit had been seen inspecting—exploded on the *James T. Staples*. Its captain was killed, along with twenty-five others.

Many more were badly injured. It was the last great steamboat accident on the rivers of Alabama.

The wounded had barely escaped the doomed vessel before it broke from its moorings and started to drift with the current downstream. By some miracle, the boat didn't sink—that is, not until it came to the shore of the Bladon Springs Cemetery, where Captain Norman Staples was buried. Then and only then did it go down, disappearing below the muddy waters forever.

They say that the spirit of the doomed captain still walks the rows of chiseled stone at Bladon Springs Cemetery. He keeps watch over the graves of his children, three of whom died before they reached their sixth birthdays. They say that his eyes are always pointed toward the river, to the spot where his greatest love waits in its final resting place.

GREENE COUNTY

Greene County, named after Revolutionary War hero Nathanael Greene of Rhode Island, was once one of the richest counties in all of Alabama. The old Rosemount Plantation is a testament to that legacy, and if local legends are to be believed, the old residents have never quite left the premises. But despite its rich legacy, Greene County is one of the poorest, per capita, in the country.

Rosemount Plantation

If you take the interstate out of Tuscaloosa down into the Black Belt, the city soon runs out, and the wilderness begins. And if you are adventurous, you may detour onto State Road 43 into Demopolis. But it is the rare traveler who steers his or her vehicle down County Road 20 into the rural wilds. And most who do and pass through the village of Forkland probably never even notice what was the crown jewel of the once wealthy county.

Rosemount Plantation, built in the Greek Rival style that we see so often in this book and in any study of the antebellum period, lies beyond the road, swallowed up by the forest. It is a testament to the transitory nature of man's stay on this globe, although perhaps it also speaks to his enduring legacy.

Williams Allen Glover built Rosemount over a two-decade period on a hill from which he could survey his three-thousand-acre plantation and where he could house his sixteen children. Down the long driveway, up the hill and past an ornamental pond passed the wealthiest and most powerful families in the South as they came to pay their respect to Glover and his accomplishments. Crowned by a cupola that is the largest in Alabama and was often used for musical entertainment, even some of the other planters who had built their own mansions must have been impressed by Rosemount at its height. The finest marble in the world—quarried from Italy and transported to Alabama—completed the majesty.

But pride goeth before the fall, and few residences that survived the war fell harder than Rosemount. The empire of cotton collapsed under its own weight, and even the wealthiest families lost everything. Those who lived in Rosemount in the years that followed became as withdrawn and reclusive as the house in which they lived. What had once been a place of grand parties and huge gatherings became an abode of mystery and legend.

At one time, several decades ago, someone purchased Rosemount and began a restoration. And yet, after pouring thousands into the house, it was suddenly and mysteriously abandoned again. For 180 years, Rosemount has stood, but now nature is retaking what is hers. Why did the owners leave? What is it about Rosemount that keeps it abandoned, even though it is one of the finest examples of antebellum architecture in the world?

In truth, so little is known about Rosemount that it is hard to say. Stories trickle out, and the residents of Greene County certainly have their legends. It is said that there was once a gallows at Rosemount, or at least that men were hanged there, perhaps from the very trees that now shade the approach to the mansion. Could it be that the spirits of these men drove away the owners of Rosemount? Are they responsible for the lights that are sometimes seen, drifting through the forest around the house? Or are there others who lived and died in Rosemount and never left?

It is impossible to know for sure, but whatever the case, Rosemount no longer belongs to the living. It is altogether the home of the past and of the dead.

HALE COUNTY

Hale County has an interesting history. It did not exist before the Civil War but rather was carved out of a number of other counties, primarily Greene. In the years that followed the war, Hale County was named after

Lieutenant Colonel Stephen F. Hale, a hero of the conflict. Hale was a leading secessionist and a signer of the constitution of the Confederate States of America. In addition to serving in the Confederate army, Hale was also an ambassador of the new nation, traveling to Kentucky in an attempt to convince the people of that state to join the Rebel cause. In that effort, he failed, and Hale would eventually meet his end as so many of the men of his generation did—dead as a result of battle wounds, a victim of the war he helped to create.

As for Hale County, it has a number of interesting characteristics. Hale County became famous when it was included in the 1941 book *Let Us Now Praise Famous Men*, by Walker Evans and James Agee, chronicling the poverty of the South during the Great Depression. It is also home to a national historic landmark of ancient pedigree, the Moundville Archaeological Park. Consisting of dozens of earthen mounds varying in size from a few yards to more than fifty feet in height, the site was the capital of a Mississippian culture about which archaeologists know almost nothing. But whatever caused the site's decline and abandonment, there are those who have spent time at Moundville and claim that the spirits of the Native Americans who once lived there never went away.

Moundville Archaeological Park

More than one thousand years ago, long before Christopher Columbus would dream of sailing the ocean blue to the Far East, before even the Normans invaded the British Isles and created the England we know today, the Mississippians came to a bluff overlooking the Black Warrior River and built one of the most magnificent cities of the age. These were the mound builders, and Moundville represented the hub of their empire.

In about AD 1000, settlers came to the land overlooking the Black Warrior and found a spot perfect for the city they wished to build. They cut down the trees and leveled the plain, creating a grand open gallery in which they could build monuments that would last for eternity. Twenty-six earthen pyramids were constructed by these people, the greatest of them rising six stories. From this place, the god-kings of the Mississippians ruled their people, made sacrifices to the beings they worshiped and commanded a trade empire that stretched for hundreds of miles. And then, five hundred years later, they vanished. By the time Hernando de Soto and his men arrived in the area, the culture had become so obscure that his chronicles do not even mention

Above: One of the Indian burial mounds. *Courtesy Karla Valentine.*

Below: Distant front view of the Moundville Museum. *Courtesy Karla Valentine.*

the great mounds. All they left behind were thousands of skeletons buried around the area and artifacts of enigmatic and unknown meaning, including perhaps the most famous of all: a great hand inscribed on an obsidian disk, with the eye of God at its center.

Moundville is also one of the most haunted places in Alabama. We know so little about the people who lived there that it is hard to say precisely why that is. But any visitor to the area who has deigned to spend the night on the nearby campgrounds would not disagree. The energy there is thick, the feeling of never being alone palpable. An oppressive mist rises from nowhere, moving against the wind, as if it were composed of a thing with a mind of its own. Orbs of light seem to float above the surface, zooming out of view if you get too close. Whispers echo across the plain, and the field is littered with cold spots, even in the heart of the summer.

Why did the ancient Indians come to this place? Where did they go? Why did they leave? These are questions that modern science has struggled to answer. Perhaps we should add this one to the list: why did they decide to come back, long after death?

The Whatley House

If there's a rule about building a house, one that we might say goes to the very foundation of home construction, it is to know the land on which you build. Practical concerns include ensuring that the soil can support the weight of the home, that it doesn't consist of "shifting sands," as it were. But you also need to know what was there before. If you don't, you just might end up building your house in the middle of a city of the dead.

J.W. Whatley built this modest, two-story frame house in 1840. It has survived to this day, acquiring some level of fame as one of the homes photographed by the Historic American Buildings Survey conducted by federal New Deal agencies in the 1930s. Much of the building's history is lost, but one thing that everyone seems to agree on is this: something strange moves through the halls of the old house. The classic signs of a haunting are all present: cold spots, the feeling of not being alone, objects that seem to misplace themselves and a general sense of unease and foreboding. But if there's no one who lives in the Whatley House who can ever truly sleep a night in peace, at least they are never lonely.

You see, a few years after Whatley built the property, they say he was resting on his front porch one day, perhaps pondering why strange things

The site of the Whatley House. *Courtesy Karla Valentine.*

always seemed to happen in his home. An old black man appeared in his drive, a recently freed man, come to visit the place where his family had lived before he was sold off to a plantation owner in another city. The look of shock and horror written on the man's face was plain as day.

"Why'd you build your house here?" the old man was said to have asked. Whatley had little patience for a black man offering him so little respect, but perhaps he could tell that this old gentleman had information that he needed to know as well, so he humored him.

"The land was cheap," he answered.

The old man pointed at the ground. "My father," he said, "is buried on this land. My grandfather, too." And as the blood flowed from Whatley's face, he continued, "This entire field is a graveyard. You're standing on the bones of dead men."

Tinker Place

She walks through the house in the gay dress of a southern lady. She warms herself by the fire. She admires the exquisite crystal and china on display. She rubs her hands along the fine-grain wood of the house. She smiles politely when she sees you. And if you speak to her, she disappears. This is Susian Truman Tinker, the matron of the Tinker Place, a woman so beloved by the community of Greensboro that she decided never to leave.

She came to the small town in 1835, determined to add a touch of class to the lives of its citizens. She built her home, and there she held grand galas for the people of Greensboro, all of whom clamored for an invitation to her parties. They were rarely disappointed, as Ms. Susian would open her home to anyone who wished it. And when she died, oh how the people of Greensboro mourned their loss. But perhaps they didn't have to. For Susian so loved the city, and she so loved her beautiful home, that she never really went away.

If you go there today and spend any time within the fine halls of the Tinker Place, you will likely meet a charming woman from another age, one who wants nothing else than to leave you completely at ease. Enjoy your evening.

Marengo County

Whatever else anybody has to say about Marengo County, one can't deny that its founders had classical antiquity on their mind when they arrived there. The name of its largest city, Demopolis, means "city of the people." Its county seat, Linden, is a shortening of "Hohenlinden," scene of a victory by the armies of Napoleon over Prussia in Bavaria in 1800. Marengo itself is the name of the location of a Napoleonic victory over the Austrians in Italy. This unusual quirk comes from the fact that the original settlers were exiled French Bonapartists who arrived in Alabama keen on establishing a so-called vine and olive colony that would produce wine and olive oil.

Unfortunately for the industrious French, the land they settled was suitable for planting neither grapevines nor olive trees. Many of the colonists migrated farther south to Mobile or New Orleans, cities that already had a high number of French inhabitants. This left a number of ghost towns behind, including Aigleville, named for the French Imperial Eagle standard that soldiers of the Grand Armée carried into battle.

Gaineswood Plantation

It's never a good time to die, but in the nineteenth century, woe be unto the man or woman who died in the winter, when the ground had frozen and the roads were covered in ice. Spades and shovels can't pierce the iron-hard ground of a January field, and a horse-drawn carriage can't carry a coffin down impassible byways.

Yes, we can approach death with rationality. Death is inevitable. Everyone you have ever known—every friend, every relative, every lover, all of them—will die. We will live to see it, to lose them all one by one—unless, of course, we die first ourselves. This is the common fate of man.

But even the rational mind must be troubled by some thoughts, and the fate of those who passed in November, December or January before the days of modern machinery must be one of those. They were dead, yes, and being dead means that nothing can harm them. But in dying so late, the dead ensured that rest was delayed. As the days would shorten, the sun flee and the trees die, the ground would freeze. There was only one thing to do, then, in the days of the nineteenth century: store the bodies and put them up somewhere for the long winter until the dirt became loose enough to turn again. And so they would sit, in a shed, underneath the basement stairs or in a storage crypt. Mouldering, rotting in the open air for the world to take note. And so the men and women of the 1800s would pray that, when death did come, they would be someplace warm.

But it was not to be for Evelyn Carter, the guest who came to the plantation of Gaineswood but never left it. Now, one might expect that a ghost might haunt a place like Gaineswood on the basis of its sheer beauty alone—this elegant mansion, with its twelve columns welcoming visitors to the portico and its beautiful gardens that surround it. But Evelyn's ghost was not one that chose to stay. She was cursed with the worst timing of all.

It was a cold winter, the coldest that the people of Demopolis could ever remember seeing, the kind of winter that southern Alabama rarely, if ever, experiences. And it was under the shadow of the steel-gray clouds, buffeted by the icy, cold wind, that Evelyn Carter passed away. The roads were frozen solid with ice, and snow covered the ground. The people of Gaineswood could neither bury her in Alabama nor transport her body to her native Virginia. And so they did all they could. They put Evelyn's body in a pine box, sealed it with pine tar and put it under the stairs in the cellar, where the cold air might preserve it. And then they went on about their lives, living with the dead corpse of a woman they all loved. And it seems that she was not at all pleased.

In the evenings that followed Evelyn's temporary entombment, the sound of footsteps coming from the cellar began to echo through the dark watches of the night. Those who live in Gaineswood began to feel a chilling presence, far colder than the winter winds. They would hear the pitter-patter of feet heading into the room where the piano is kept, the piano that Evelyn had loved to play during her life. And from that room would come the sweet strains of music, even when no one was around. How did they know the room was empty? Because when they would enter the chamber, the music would cease and the guilty culprit would be nowhere to be found.

They buried Evelyn that spring. One might have expected the footsteps, the whispers and the music to stop. But it seems that Evelyn simply went without a proper burial for too long. Gaineswood is haunted by her spirit to this day.

The Eliza Battle

It was an age of excess, wealth and decadence. Cotton was king, and the planters of the South were rich beyond their wildest dreams. And perhaps nothing brings to mind the glory of that age like the riverboat. With the South poorly connected by rails at that time, the rivers were the great highways and byways. Much as today, goods moved in abundance up and down these watery roads, but so, too, did people. Like the great Atlantic liners of the early twentieth century, the men and women who traveled in these magnificent paddle-wheel boats did so in the utmost style. And like the *Titanic* fifty years later, when the belle of the Tombigbee met its end, it did so spectacularly.

It was its maiden voyage of the year 1858, and as such, it was one of the great events in the river culture of that time. It was a floating party, a river-bound ballroom. Music played day and night. Men and women danced and laughed and ate and drank. And none of them knew the fate that awaited them down the river way.

As these things tend to go when the water goes bad and turns from friend to foe, it started with a ship heavily laden with cargo and passengers, as well as a night that was bitterly cold. Beyond the fire-lit halls where the men and women danced, the air had turned frigid and the rain to sleet. No one knows how it started. Maybe it was a crewman huddled around a flame, struggling to stay warm. Maybe it was the spark from a fire within the boiler room. But whatever it was, a cry went up from within the boat: "Fire!"

Shouts of joy turned to howls of chaos. Men and women threw themselves from the deck into the freezing river below, desperate to escape the catastrophe. Some of them found themselves in places where they could not climb out of the icy water. They clung to trees, crying for help, until the air froze their limbs, and they fell into the depths below to drown.

The captain, doing everything in his power to save his passengers and crew, attempted to send the boat full speed ahead into the shoreline. But before he could turn the boat completely, the ropes that controlled his steering snapped. Now the boat was flying through the water as fast as it could go, and it was completely out of control.

What a sight it must have been, the *Eliza Battle*, thundering down the river like a hellhound aflame, night turning to day, fire leaping from its decks, whistles blowing and calliope playing maniacally. On it went, until the ship itself was little more than a ball of flaming fury. Only when the river took it did the fire die into the last wisps of a column of smoke.

Eighty men and women died that night. Another hundred bore the scars of frozen limbs and burnt skin for all their days. It was the worst

The Tombigbee River. *Photo by David Higdon.*

disaster in the history of the Tombigbee River. Thus was the end of the *Eliza Battle*. Or was it?

The tales started as whispers shared among the men who plied their trade by the muddy waters of the Tombigbee. It floated with the river from one small-town dock to the next, growing in fervor as it did. Those whispers turned to open talk, and that talk gradually acquired the strength of legend and myth. For whatever the truth may be, those who live along the river say that the *Eliza Battle* still makes its way down the Tombigbee, a vision of horror and a harbinger of doom. For when you see that fireball from hell racing with the current on cold and windy nights, when you hear the screams of the damned and their pitiful cries for help, death is on your very doorstep.

PICKENS COUNTY

Pickens County has one of the most famous haunted locations in Alabama: the Pickens County Courthouse. Pickens was one of the few counties in Alabama to suffer real damage during the Civil War, with Northern troops burning the old courthouse to the ground. Its replacement was also burned to the ground only a few years later. And it was this incident that would eventually cause the events that would make Pickens County famous in paranormal circles worldwide. But while the courthouse has a story unlike any other, it is not the only haunted location in the small county.

Pickens County Courthouse

There is a courthouse in the tiny town of Carrollton that is perhaps the most famous of any in the South—maybe the whole country. How did the blandly named Pickens County Courthouse in a village of less than one thousand people gain such renown?

Falkner once said that the past isn't dead; it isn't even past. And in the South, that axiom burns with truth. Why is the courthouse in Pickens County famous? It was something that happened long ago, beginning with the final days of the Civil War.

The South burned. From Richmond in the north to Atlanta in the south and all points west, the flames of Yankee anger scorched clean the once proud cities of the Confederacy. It was all done as a matter of military necessity, of course. Or so the soldiers who lit the fires would say. But everyone knew by April 1865 that the war was over and the South had been defeated. Four years of bloody Civil War had fostered its share of hatred, and no one was quite ready to let bygones be bygones. The dead could not be brought back, but they could be avenged.

And so, when General Croxton's Raiders came to Carrollton, they looked for something to destroy. Even though it served no military purpose whatsoever, their angry eyes fell on the courthouse in the center of town. The desperate people of the tiny hamlet—already bone tired and beat down from the depravations of war—pleaded with the soldiers to spare the old structure, but to no avail. Torches were lit, and the building was burned to the ground.

But something stirred in the people of Carrollton then, a sense of determination that no invader could conquer. They had no money. They had no supplies. They had no skilled labor. And yet they decided that they would rebuild the courthouse, no matter what it took. Under the mocking and doubt-filled gaze of occupying soldiers, the people of Carrollton began to rebuild. And somehow, they were successful. They opened the courthouse with great fanfare, and it became a symbol of a reconstructing South that would not let the defeat of war forever crush its spirit.

For more than a decade, the courthouse stood, becoming the center of life in the tiny town. The people of Carrolton loved the place, and so when in 1877 the courthouse caught fire and followed the path of its predecessor, burning to the ground, the residents of Pickens County were heartbroken. That sorrow turned to burning anger when an investigation revealed that the fire had begun in several places at once, the sure sign of an arsonist.

For weeks, the investigation dragged on, so long that a new courthouse (less grand and more functional) was built while the parties responsible for the destruction of the old one were still on the loose. And with every hot summer day that passed, the people of Carrollton grew more and more impatient with the authorities. Rumblings began to grow that the police were incompetent, and more than one Carrolltonian decided to take matters into his own hands. They began to search for a suspect, and more than that, they began to search for a scapegoat.

It is an unfortunate characteristic of human beings that when bad things happen and we don't know who is responsible, we look for someone to blame. And too often, that blame falls on an outsider, a stranger we already suspect. This was the fate of Henry Wells.

Let it be stated clearly: Henry Wells was no angel. In fact, most people would have thought him closer to a devil in character. He was a drifter, a known brawler who was said to carry a knife with him wherever he went, a blade he was not shy about using. But perhaps most importantly in the postwar South when racism was in no short supply, Henry Wells was black. And in the minds of some members of the community, that was a recipe for just the kind of man who would have burned down their courthouse. Plans were laid to seek revenge on Wells, and a lynching party was formed. A posse of men rode out into the night to find Wells and enact its brand of justice.

The sheriff of the town got wind of what was happening. He was no fan of Wells, but he knew that there was little, if any, evidence that he was responsible for what happened at to the old courthouse. He found Wells before the posse could, and he took him back to the new courthouse for his protection.

Unfortunately for everyone involved, it's hard to keep a secret in a town the size of Carrollton, and before Wells or the sheriff could catch his breath, the posse was at the courthouse steps, demanding that Wells be turned over to it for its own brand of justice. The sheriff took Wells high into the

Interior view of the Pickens Courthouse. *Photo by David Higdon.*

courthouse and hid him in a garret on the very top floor. There he told Wells to hide and stay quiet. Then he went downstairs to face the crowd.

There on the porch in front of the building, Wells's fate would be decided, and he knew it. Curiosity got the better of him. He had to hear what they were saying. He had to know if the sheriff's pleas were falling on deaf ears. So, he crawled across the floor and looked out one of the windows to the crowd below.

A storm was settling in, and what had been distant thunder now became a portent of an imminent downpour. Wells watched the crowd below, but then someone looked up at the high window in the garret. He saw Wells and pointed. Now they were all looking at him. Their quarry brought to ground, there was no cajoling by the sheriff that would stop them now. Wells knew it, too. He cried out to the men below, "I'm innocent! If you kill me, I'll haunt this town as long as it stands!"

It's here that consensus breaks down on what happened in Carrollton all those years ago. But one thing all agree on is that as the words were leaving Wells's mouth, they were sealed with a lightning bolt from the heavens. Some say that the bolt actually struck Wells, killing him dead in an act that the townspeople took as divine judgment on a man who had tempted God one too many times. Others say that the bolt simply struck the building but did not kill Wells. That was left to the posse, which had already begun to storm the building as Wells was speaking. The people dragged him from the garret and took him to the outskirts of town. As the rain beat down and the lightning flashed around them, they hanged Wells until he was good and dead.

But whatever happened that night, everyone knows what occurred the next morning. As the sun rose and the clouds broke, one of the men of the posse was looking up at the courthouse garret where Wells had hidden. Suddenly, he was struck with terror, falling down to the ground and weeping. Others followed his eyes to where his gaze had been. There, in the garret window where Wells had looked out at the death posse below was a face, as clear as day. An image, burned into the pane of glass by the bolt of lightning. The image of the terrified visage of Wells, an eternal reminder of what the town had done, just as Wells had promised.

Dozens of times, men have tried to wash that image away—especially the sheriff, who saw it as a constant reminder of his failure. But no matter how many times they tried, and no matter what cleaning agent they used, every effort was made in vain. Over the years, Carrollton has been struck with the violent storms that often rock the Black Belt region. Hail has pounded

Henry Wells's ghostly image in the bottom-right panel. *Photo by David Higdon.*

Front view of the Pickens County Courthouse. *Photo by David Higdon.*

the courthouse, and throughout the decades, every single window has been broken at one time or another. All but one—that very pane.

He's there to this day. You can see it if you go to Carrollton and look up to the high garret window to the pane on the bottom right-hand side. And if you listen closely on nights when the electric tingle of a storm is in the air, you are liable to hear a voice that seems to come from high above you whisper, "I'm innocent!"

Reform Medical Hospital

In 1947, there was a hopeful feeling in Pickens County, Alabama. The long world war was over. Peace and prosperity had returned to our shores, and a new hospital was to be built in the city of Reform—a town famously named for the last word of a preacher as he fled the hell-raising town, "Reform!" In 1953, after six years of hard work, planning and no shortage of fundraising, the hospital was opened to great fanfare.

But there was a problem. In their exuberance for providing good medical care to the people of the area, the authorities had actually built two hospitals, one in Reform and one in nearby Aliceville. Within three years, financial difficulties began to emerge. There simply wasn't enough money available to professionally staff and equip two hospitals. When a feasibility study was finally conducted in 1967, it was determined that one hospital would be much better than two. In a moment of mathematical brilliance, the study determined that reducing the county's hospitals from two to one would result in a savings of approximately 50 percent.

Groundbreaking ceremonies were not held until 1977, with the doors to the new hospital opening in 1979. And that was the end for the Reform hospital, one that had started with such hopes and served the county for thirty years. It was left to fall to ruin in the wilds of Pickens County, with nothing but its memories and the ghosts that haunt it to keep it company—for ghosts there are. Like any hospital, Reform saw great joy and great sorrow in the days its doors were open. It saw plenty of new life, but it also saw untold death. And the dead do not always go quietly.

Reform Hospital is not a particularly safe place to visit anymore, but that doesn't keep teenagers, paranormal investigators and the just plain curious from doing so. And what they say they encounter within the halls is quite remarkable. Witnesses report that the halls are filled with disembodied apparitions, appearing as shadow people that walk throughout the hospital

Room 102 of the Old Reform Hospital. *Photo by David Higdon.*

oblivious to those who would observe. Other spirits seem to have gone in another direction altogether, with some claiming to have seen balls of light floating through the morgue of the hospital, often approaching to within inches of the witness's face. The nursery still echoes with the sound of babies crying, and through the mold and dust and decay floats the smell of sterile bandages and disinfectant.

The Reform Hospital may have closed long ago, but it is still alive with spiritual activity.

SUMTER COUNTY

Sumter County is home to the University of West Alabama, once known as Livingston after the city that is the county seat. This sleepy little town has a delightfully haunted history, one dominated by a singular figure from the area: Julia Tutwiler. In addition to having written the state song of Alabama, Tutwiler was an educator of some renown. She was the first and only female president of the University of West Alabama, and it was through her efforts that the University of Alabama admitted women in 1892. In addition to being known as the "mother of co-education," she was also considered the "angel of the prisons" for her reforms of the Alabama prison system. All in all, a remarkable story for a woman from the late nineteenth century. If some are to be believed, that story is still being written, as Tutwiler has been known to roam the halls of Tutwiler Library at West Alabama, or the Lakewood House, depending on whom you believe.

Julia Tutwiler Library at the University of West Alabama

The first place that may lay claim to the spirit of Julia Tutwiler is the library that bears her name at the University of West Alabama, formerly known as Livingston. A painting of this famous and accomplished woman hangs in a place of honor within the building. That's helpful, as it is said that if you visit the library late at night, after the students have gone home and a quiet has fallen over the place, you just might see a spirit floating among the stacks. The ghost is described as a woman, elderly, dressed in the wardrobe of the late nineteenth century. She is a kindly old woman, and no one has ever claimed to have experienced any ill feeling from her presence. Everyone who has ever seen her believes that she is the spirit of Julia Tutwiler.

Does Tutwiler haunt the library at the University of West Alabama? It is true that she spent many years at the school, and although she traveled far and wide, it is doubtful that she ever loved a place as much as West Alabama. But the school is not the only locale that claims her.

Lakewood House

The other place Julia may have made her permanent abode is the Lakewood House, a historic antebellum mansion. This two-and-a-half-story Greek Revival–style house was completed in 1840 by Joseph Lake, who had moved to Alabama from North Carolina. By coincidence, Julia Tutwiler was actually related to Lake, and she lived in the house from 1881 to 1910 while president of Livingston.

That there is a spirit that haunts Lakewood is not much denied. But whether or not it is Julia Tutwiler is less certain. The family who lived in the Lakewood house always described it as a friendly, comforting spirit. More than one visitor, upon noticing an unexplained presence passing by the window—most often it seemed when they were eating (perhaps the spirit is hungry)—would be met with the remark, "No, that's just our ghost."

Everyone seems to be in agreement on the form of the spirit: it is seen almost universally as a wisp of white floating by. Is this the ghost of Julia Tutwiler? It's hard to say, although the white ghost is not the only spirit to haunt Lakewood. Some of the others are nowhere near as friendly. One of the children who lived in the house reported a strange encounter when she was visiting from college. She was cleaning up when she had the distinct impression that she was being watched. Out of the corner of her eye, she saw a man, dressed in a red, plaid flannel shirt. But when she turned, there was nothing there beyond a sinking feeling in the pit of her stomach.

In fact, Lakewood may well be one of the most haunted places in all of Alabama. One visitor reported waking to the sight of the ghostly figures of a woman and a child standing nearby. Others have experienced playful spirits that turn the lights on and off while they are in the shower. Rocking chairs rock on their own. Cameras take photographs without warning. Strange lights float about the house. Innumerable spiritual orbs have been reported.

Who haunts Lakewood? No one knows for sure, but no one doubts that the house has a resident spirit, and perhaps more than one.

The Alamuchee-Bellamy Covered Bridge

There's just something about covered bridges. It was a covered bridge that ended the power of the Headless Horseman in "The Legend of Sleepy Hollow," and it is covered bridges that are often the source of paranormal stories throughout the country. So it is with the Alamuchee-Bellamy Covered Bridge in Livingston, Alabama.

Built in 1861 by Confederate army captain William Alexander Campbell Jones, the bridge was a valuable crossing for Confederate forces led by General Nathan Bedford Forrest in their efforts to reinforce beleaguered defenders in Mississippi. Despite being a critical piece of infrastructure for the Rebel cause, it somehow survived the Civil War. It was finally closed to motor traffic in 1958 and moved to its current location as a crossing over the Duck Pond on the campus of the University of West Alabama.

But the ghost that is said to haunt the bridge dates from a time in the decades following the Civil War. Perhaps the most famous man ever to live in Livingston was Stephen S. Renfroe, known as Alabama's Outlaw

Sheriff. He is said to have been a Confederate army deserter who managed to avoid the wrath of the authorities. He married three times, murdering his first brother-in-law and watching as his wives died under "mysterious circumstances." In 1878, he managed to somehow become the sheriff of Sumter County. But Renfroe had no desire to enforce the law. He wanted to use his position to take advantage of the people. He became the leader of the Ku Klux Klan in the area. He launched attacks against occupying Union troops, sparked several riots and murdered two Republican politicians, one white and one black. But when his exploits began to include theft, rape and general debauchery, the local people turned against him.

He was arrested, but he used his connections to escape. It was his first prison break. But it wouldn't be his last. By some accounts, he escaped prison more than a dozen times, with each attempt more daring than the last. For six years, he was on the run, a member of several gangs, always managing to survive longer than the rest of the group's members. Finally, he made the mistake of returning to Sumter County. There he was once again arrested, but the people made sure that he had no chance to escape. A lynch mob was formed, and the old sheriff was taken down to the Alamuchee-Bellamy Covered Bridge and hanged from it. His reign of terror was over. Or was it?

They say that the night does not rest easy around the old covered bridge. A figure is seen walking its length, one that is as insubstantial as it is paranormal—a shadow wreathed in darkness. They even say that there's a black-and-white cat that stalks the bridge, vanishing into nothing. And always there is a feeling of cold and emptiness, as if there is no life on the bridge, no hope. Only death.

WASHINGTON COUNTY

Washington County is named after the first president of the United States. Ironically, given that act of patriotism, Washington County was also one of the most enthusiastic supporters of the Confederate cause. More than three quarters of the men in Washington County volunteered to fight for the Confederate army.

Washington County is the oldest county in Alabama, and it witnessed one of the most unusual and sensational events in the history of the nation. For it was in this county in the old territorial capital of St. Stephens—now a ghost town—that Aaron Burr was arrested.

Aaron Burr was a colorful character, to say the least. Burr lived a rather charmed life during the early part of his career. He served bravely as a Continental army soldier during the Revolutionary War. He was successful both as a lawyer and a politician, and he served in the New York State Assembly and as attorney general. His meteoric rise continued when he was selected to be a United States senator. And then, in 1801, he became Thomas Jefferson's vice president after failing—through political chicanery that would make a modern politician blush—to secure the nation's highest office. That failure had much to do with the machinations of Alexander Hamilton.

Hamilton had long been suspicious of Burr's seemingly endless political ambition, including his belief that Burr would do anything to seize control of New York (even join a secessionist movement). Hamilton was not shy about airing those views, and Burr got wind of the charges. Burr demanded an apology. Hamilton refused to give it. Thus, Burr demanded satisfaction of his honor in the way of a duel.

The duel took place in New York, on the same site where Hamilton's son was killed in an earlier duel, even using the same weapon that killed him. Hamilton was determined to secure his honor. He was also determined to end Burr's political career. There was one way to do both. Hamilton fired his shot high, missing intentionally. Burr shot Hamilton in the stomach, mortally wounding him. Hamilton died with the legacy of a national hero and one of the great Founding Fathers. Burr became an outcast.

But that didn't mean that his political career was finished, at least not in his mind. Any path to power along the ordinary lines was utterly lost to him. Although he fled to South Carolina, his remaining duties as vice president required that he return to Washington. As for New York and New Jersey, those states he was forced to avoid, as warrants for his arrest for murder were issued in both jurisdictions. In any event, Jefferson wanted nothing to do with Burr, and when his first term was over, Burr was replaced.

Burr went to the West, and while in the state of Ohio, he concocted a half-formed plan to foment a war with Spain and use the occasion to seize large tracts of land from that nation that he would then rule as his own private fiefdom. Burr gathered around him army officers, landholders and politicians who had much to gain from a war with Spain. In Louisiana, he convinced a number of settlers who were eager for that war—including the bishop of New Orleans—that he intended to invade Mexico. To the Mexican ambassador, he claimed an intention of marching on Washington, much to the pleasure of officials in Madrid. Spain was so optimistic about the possibility that the United States might split in two that it funded part of Burr's efforts.

Unfortunately for Burr, he trusted the wrong people. His chief ally, General James Wilkinson—for whom Burr had secured the governorship of the Louisiana Territory—betrayed Burr to Jefferson. His base in Ohio was overrun by the territorial militia, and Jefferson declared Burr a traitor. Burr's men surrendered when they learned of the bounty on their leader's head, but he escaped into the wilderness. It was then that Burr and Washington County became bound together, as it was in the town of Wakefield that he was finally captured in 1807.

Burr was tried before Chief Justice John Marshall and represented by Edmund Randolph, the first United States attorney general. Jefferson threw all of his efforts into convicting Burr, but the standard for treason is quite high—a conviction could only hold if two witnesses testified to the deed. In a testament to the legitimacy of the fledgling nation's justice system, Burr was acquitted.

But his days of public life were finished. He fled to Europe, and even though he would return to America years later, he lived out his days in relative obscurity. And he never returned to Alabama.

St. Stephens

St. Stephens is a ghost town. To walk its empty streets and look on its deserted ruins, one would never know that it was once the capital of Alabama.

St. Stephens is one of the oldest settlements in all of Alabama. Founded in the 1700s by the Spanish, it quickly became a mecca for the men and women moving into the Alabama territory. By the early 1800s, it had been recognized as both a strategic location and as a key trading post along the Tombigbee River. It was to the fort at St. Stephens that Aaron Burr was taken when he was captured. Soon, St. Stephens was a boomtown, and in 1817, it was named the territorial capital of the soon-to-be state. With its fame and wealth came decadence and corruption.

In a letter to President Thomas Jefferson, Ephraim Kirby said of the residents of St. Stephens, "[They are] illiterate, wild and savage, of depraved morals, unworthy of public confidence or private esteems, litigious, disunited, and knowing each other, universally distrustful of each other." It is said that St. Stephens had more than fifty licensed taverns—with scores more operating under the table—but not a single

Front view of the St. Stephens Courthouse. *Courtesy Lee Peacock.*

church. It was to this lawless, godless place that famed pioneer preacher Lorenzo Dow came.

To the people of St. Stephens, Dow preached a sermon of condemnation, calling on them to repent their sinful ways before it was too late. How did the people of St. Stephens respond? They took Lorenzo Dow, tarred and feathered him and sent him off on a raft down the river. It is said that as they jeered and laughed at the old preacher, he stood in the raft and pointed to the town. And then he cursed it. "The day will come," he is reported to have said, "when St. Stephens will be nothing but a roosting place for bats and owls, when no stone will lie upon another." No doubt the people of St. Stephens, if they thought on the words of Lorenzo at all, did so only to mock him. But the days of St. Stephens were already numbered.

First, the governor and the assemblymen of the state legislature conspired to move the capital to a more central location, choosing Cahawba as the new seat of government. Then, developments in riverboat technology allowed the tradesmen to bypass St. Stephens altogether, delivering their goods all the way to Mobile. An epidemic of yellow fever followed this indignity, decimating the population. Within a few years, much of the populace had moved to New St. Stephens, a town a few miles away that was served by the railroad. There they built the beautiful St. Stephens Courthouse in the hopes of perhaps drawing people back to the area. But they never came. By the time the Civil War was over, St. Stephens was abandoned completely, its only residents the bats and the owls that made the old ruined buildings their homes.

Thus was the curse fulfilled.

WILCOX COUNTY

Like so many of the counties in Alabama, Wilcox was named after a soldier who lost his life in the Creek War. It is a tiny county with a rather impoverished population, but that does not mean it is without stories of the long dead.

Snow Hill Institute

While the Civil War may have ended slavery, it didn't end discrimination against African Americans—not by a long shot. And so, while former slaves had their freedom, they did not have equal opportunity. That included opportunities to acquire a good education. Fortunately, there were some men who saw further than others. One of those men was Booker T. Washington, the founder of Tuskegee University. And it was a graduate of that school, Dr. William J. Edwards, who was the mind behind the Colored Literary and Industrial School, soon to be known as the Snow Hill Institute.

It began with an idea. Edwards, upon graduating from Tuskegee, returned to the plantation on which he was born, inspired by the motto of his class ("Deeds, not words"). And in R.O. Simpson, the owner of the plantation and generations of Edwards's ancestors, he found a man who had similar ideas. Simpson had been inspired to improve the lot of the men and women who had once served him and his family as slaves. Edwards and Simpson got together, and the first building of Snow Hill was a small log cabin on seven acres of Simpson's land. That turned into thirty-three acres and then one hundred. In later years, the school would buy north of half of the plantation—nearly two thousand acres. During it all, Simpson and his family were consummate allies of the school. Three students grew to four hundred, with a staff of thirty-five working out of twenty-seven buildings.

Edwards, who incidentally is the grandfather of filmmaker Spike Lee, ran the school for many years, but its legacy outlived him. Not only was Snow Hill Institute a place of education, it was also a home for racial reconciliation as well. Famous men like Dr. George Washington Carver would come to speak in the grand auditorium at Snow Hill. And when they did, whites and blacks from the community would gather together as equals to hear them.

Unfortunately, it would not always be so. The fight against Jim Crow and segregation was not without its unintended casualties, and Snow Hill was one of them. In 1973, desegregation orders mandated that black students be bused into white schools so that these facilities could establish some modicum of racial integration. When they did, the student body of Snow Hill was gradually siphoned away until there weren't enough students left to maintain the institution. In 1973, the school closed, leaving behind the founder's home, five teachers' cottages, the library and a few other buildings as the only physical reminders of the school's existence. But the memories still remain.

There are many stories of restless spirits that remain at Snow Hill. One student came all the way from Boston to get a quality education, but she never quite acclimated to the very different world of south Alabama. Unfortunately, her depression soon deepened terribly. One day, she walked to the river that ran beside the school and threw herself into the rushing waters. Before anyone could save her, she had drowned. To this day, if you go down to the little creek beside the school, you can hear the sound of sobbing coming from the banks of the river.

Other spirits are more corporeal. Spike Lee's father would hunt in the forests around the school. One day, while he was hunting for raccoons, he came upon a tree where he thought the 'coon had fled. But when the dogs arrived at the tree, they ran away, their tails between their legs. The young boy, perhaps despite his better instincts, walked up to the tree. And there, sitting in its branches, was an apparition, staring down at him. Needless to say, he didn't stay behind long to figure out what exactly it was.

There's also a graveyard on the outskirts of the school. One day, a few students guided an oxen-driven carriage down to the railroad tracks to deliver some wood. The path crossed through that graveyard. The delivery took longer than they expected, and by the time they returned, the sun had set and darkness had fallen. When the oxen got to the entrance to the graveyard, they stopped dead in their tracks. No amount of coaxing would get them to move forward. Eventually, the boys gave up, leaving the oxen there for the night. When they returned the next morning, the oxen were still there, frozen in place. But as soon as the sun crested above the trees, the oxen finally marched forward.

The graveyard—one dedicated to the slaves who once worked the land around the school—has its share of tales associated with it. Sudden storms seem to fall upon the cemetery with terrible violence. Ghostly shadows seem to pass between the gravestones, and full-bodied apparitions regularly appear to visitors.

Like so many places in the Black Belt, history is thick around the ruins of the old school at Snow Hill. And it is a history that should not be forgotten. The road to equality began at places like Snow Hill. The memories of that struggle are still fresh.

The Unfilled Hole

In Wilcox County in the city of Camden sits a courthouse. And next to the courthouse, a great tree stands. The courthouse was built only a few years before the Civil War in the Greek Revival style that was popular throughout the antebellum South. The massive, columned building is one of only six antebellum courthouses still in use in the South. That history includes a number of public executions. And that is where the tree comes in.

The spot where these executions were once conducted sits in front of the Camden Public Library, which is currently located in the old courthouse. There's a pecan tree that grows on the site of those public killings, but that's not the only physical reminder of those days. There's a hole there, one that the county has tried to fill many times, to no success. In fact, such is the county's frustration with its inability to remove this open danger that it has now placed a metal warning post next to it to keep people from falling in.

Not that it is all that needed. The air is unnaturally cold there, and the whispers of the dead are always close. But that's how it is in Alabama's Black Belt. History is always nearby, and the past does not let go easily. Time stands still in the region, and if you let yourself go, you'll end up back in days long gone by, part of a past no more substantial than the voices on the wind.

Sources and Interviews

A project like this would have been impossible without the help of countless men and women who have passed down these stories throughout the generations. We spoke to many of them during our research. Some wanted to remain anonymous, while others were willing to go on the record. Their voices are here, within these pages. We thank them all, especially those mentioned below.

Interviews

Bradford, Berry. Interview on November 2, 2012, regarding the Pickens County Courthouse.

Casey, Deborah. Interview on June 26, 2013, regarding Fendall Hall.

Fazekas, Beth. Interview on June 5, 2013, regarding the Reform Medical Hospital.

Parnell, Jean. Interview on June 26, 2013, regarding the St. Stephens Courthouse.

Peacock, Lee. Interview on December 19, 2012, regarding the L&N Railroad Tunnel.

———. Interview on December 19, 2012, regarding the McConnico Cemetery.

———. Interview on December 19, 2012, regarding the Old Courthouse Museum.

———. Interview on February 11, 2013, regarding the Old Carter Hospital.
———. Interview on February 11, 2013, regarding the Castleberry Bank Building.
Perrin, Joyce. Interview on October 17, 2012, regarding the Josephine Hotel.
Serafin, Faith. Interview on April 3, 2013, regarding the Bullock County Courthouse.
———. Interview on April 3, 2013, regarding the Pauly Jail.
———. Interview on June 25, 2013, regarding the Cobb Hospital.
———. Interview on June 25, 2013, regarding the Phenix City.

Other Sources

Alabama Department of Archives and History. http://www.archives.state.al.us.
Alabama Ghost Trail. http://www.youtube.com/user/AlabamasGhostTrail.
Alabama's Front Porches. http://alabamasfrontporches.org.
Encyclopedia.com. http://www.encyclopedia.com.
The Encyclopedia of Alabama. http://www.encyclopediaofalabama.org/face/Home.jsp.
Haunted America. http://hauntingreview.com.
Haunted America Tours. http://www.hauntedamericatours.com.
Rootsweb. http://www.rootsweb.ancestry.com.
Tuscaloosa Paranormal Research Group. http://tuscaloosaparanormal.com.
Wikipedia. http://www.wikipedia.org.
Windham, Kathryn Tucker, and Margaret Gillis Figh. *13 Alabama Ghosts and Jeffrey*. Tuscaloosa: University of Alabama Press, 1969.

About the Authors

David Higdon is, above all, a father of four girls and husband of a wonderful wife for ten years. He is also the founder and lead investigator for Tuscaloosa Paranormal Research Group and a proud member of the TAPS Family (of Syfy's *Ghost Hunters*). Currently employed with a civil engineering company in Tuscaloosa, David also serves with his Alabama Army National Guard unit in Jasper, Alabama. He has served honorably overseas, including a deployment in 2004 to Iraq, where he served at FOB Normandy. He was also deployed for Operation Vigilant Relief (Hurricane Katrina).

David's passion, however, is researching the world of the paranormal. All of his life, he has heard stories of the unknown world, and it sparked something within him to find the truth, whatever that may be. He believes that there is so much out there to explore, and he wants to be a part of the learning curve that this journey may have in store for him.

A native of the South, Brett Talley received philosophy and history degrees from the University of Alabama before moving to witch-haunted Massachusetts to attend Harvard Law School. When people ask, Brett tells them that he writes for fortune and glory. But the truth is, the stories in his head simply refuse to stay put. Brett loves every kind of book—from horror to literary to historical to sci-fi—as long as there are fantastic characters with a compelling purpose. There's still magic to be found in fiction, the mysterious and the unknown still beckon there and the light can always triumph over the darkness, no matter how black the night may be. Brett's first book, *That Which Should Not Be*, was critically acclaimed and earned a Bram Stoker Nomination for Superior Achievement in a First Novel. He is also the author of *The Void*, *Limbus, Inc.* and *Haunted Tuscaloosa* with David Higdon.

Brett writes when he can, although he spends most of his time working as a lawyer so he can put food on the table. That is, until the air grows cool and crisp and fall descends. For then it is football time in the South, and Brett lives and dies with the Alabama Crimson Tide. Roll Tide.